OVER
EMPLOYED

The digital workers' revolution redefining
business as usual in the remote work age

by Rob Hockney

"Because jobs don't love you back"

"Thank you."

To the many people who shared their stories, allowed me to interrogate the details, and helped me bring this complex topic to the wider world.

All names have been changed to protect the author legally and emotionally.

Rob Hackney

PROLOGUE

At 7:00 a.m. Steve Miller's alarm clock shatters the early morning silence. Miller—a pseudonym for which the necessity will soon become obvious—is historically a prolific snoozer of alarms, though has more recently become conditioned never to let himself lie in bed a minute longer than budgeted. Steve now knows how much his time is worth: at least twice as much as the average man, based on some back of the napkin math.

Steve's mornings are a meticulously crafted routine, rigidly monitored and maintained to balance two full-time jobs that both profess to demand his undivided attention.

The aroma of freshly brewed coffee fills the air as he sits at his kitchen table, glancing at a planner with both red and purple columns. Every minute of Steve's day is accounted for in these two swim lanes—a delicate balancing act between dual lives as a web developer for a scrappy startup, and a project manager for one of the world's most hated multinationals.

By 8:00 a.m. Steve is seated at his desk, surrounded by an array of monitors and laptops, each a portal into the different facets of his professional existence.

His first job's (J1) morning stand-up meeting begins in a few minutes on one screen, while his second job's (J2) project

4

kickoff call looms on another, threatening that the host has been notified of Steve's arrival.

This overlap isn't frequent, but it happens often enough that Steve has honed a strategy for navigating the treacherous waters. Today the stakes are a little higher: crucial updates on a major client project on one call, and an essential team alignment that may require his input on the other.

As the seconds tick down, Steve's heart rate quickens. His startup colleagues appear on the left laptop screen, one face at a time, all eager and ready to dive into sprint planning, like some twisted YCombinator Brady Bunch.

On the right, the project team from his corporate job also appear in successive boxes. He sees a mixture of familiar faces and new, the revolving-door assortment of "business development" graduates and temps, consultants, whatevers that give the second role an air of impermanence that suits Steve fine. Like the first cohort of who careses—another lumping of people he will interact with in friendly ways until suddenly he doesn't anymore, never to see or think of them all again—as a group they're equally demanding and ever-presently aware of his attention, poised to discuss the launch a software feature about to go live.

To Steve they all look like obstacles. Potential hurdles, and pitfalls. A thorny question or snide remark seeking out the weakest member of the herd. For some reason, whenever he's waiting for these calls to kick off, he can't help thinking of an interaction he had in early primary school. A little troublemaker who liked to sound tough who said to him, perfectly matter-of-fact and entirely unsolicited, while waiting for a school assembly to begin: "You know, if you and me were scuba diving, and I saw a shark, I'd just slit your throat and swim away. It'd be so busy eating you, it wouldn't worry about me." That conversation came to inform so much of Steve's worldview, he now realises. He also credits that outlook to his overemployment success.

The tension in the room is palpable. Steve can feel the weight of expectation pressing down on him from both sides—a vice grip of unaddressed need for his feigned, performative focus.

His hands are steady, finger hovering over touchpad, its pointer locked to the mute button. Steve's mind races, calculating the odds of being called upon by either set of agitators. Models scenarios where these two things occur simultaneously. It's all a high-stakes game of digital brinkmanship, and he is, for now at least, the calm centre at the eye of the storm.

Steve thinks of Jack Bauer, Jack Reacher, Jack Ryan. All the good ones. Just handling it all in the field, dodging bullets while reporting back and thinking on their feet. Master of his domain. Legendary operator. Be like Jack, Steve wills himself. Any of them. All of them. Become Jack.

"Steve, any updates on the client project?" asks his startup manager, her voice clear and insistent through the left earbud.

Simultaneously, his corporate project lead crackles to life on the right, "Steve, can you walk us through the timeline for your three deliverables?"

A bead of sweat forms at his temple. This is the moment every overemployment aficionado prepares for. Will he screw it up? Wait, is he already screwing it up? Just monologuing like this while they're all there waiting, staring him down with unmet expectations? Do something, Steve. Say something, you pointless turd! Jack! Be Jack! Stop narrating and—

With a quick, practiced motion, he dual wields the two laptop touchpads to unmute both microphones simultaneously. His heart pounds, reverberating through the airbuds.

"Ah... I have that for you, but I'd like to catch up offline about a few caveats first," he says, his voice a model of calm and conviction. On this brief, simple statement lays the house of cards that is Steve's entire professional reputation.

Seconds stretch into moments. On the left screen, his manager nods, satisfied with his apparent engagement. On the right, his team continues their discussion, unfazed by what is, at best, an objectively ambiguous brush-off.

Relief floods across Steve as he quickly re-mutes both calls, leaning back in his chair, exhaling the breath he didn't know he was holding.

OVEREMPLOYED

For the next thirty minutes—the duration of both meetings—
Steve will appear to listen while comprehensively reading
every review of the mountain bike he intends to purchase,
secure in the knowledge that he has earned it.

███ ███

CHAPTER 1

RISE OF THE OVEREMPLOYED

Since around the time of the industrial revolution, we've held onto the belief as a society that a single "good job," with a steady paycheck and decent benefits, is the bedrock of financial security. More recently, that notion has begun to unravel, as people question, "What does a 'good job' even mean today?"

Over the last decade, a subtle shift has reshaped how people think about work, financial independence, and the best way to leverage their skills. Even before the pandemic, stable, long-term career roles were on the decline. As these positions dwindled, the term "gig economy" became part of everyday language, coinciding with a troubling corporate trend: executives increasingly leaning into workforce cuts as a quick way to spike quarterly numbers and secure their bonuses, without regard for long-term consequences such as brain drain, decreased employee morale, and general feelings of job insecurity across sectors and disciplines.

Overemployment feels, in essence, like the natural response to the new paradigm. It's redefining work-life balance by introducing a new way for people to stack jobs, helping them to reach career and financial goals more rapidly.

The overemployment movement wasn't designed by executives or think tanks; it developed organically, driven by the collective experience of ordinary workers. In the beginning, the idea of holding down multiple full-time jobs was an isolated survival tactic. But as stories and strategies spread online, overemployment emerged as an informal network of shared knowledge and support.

Online platforms such as Reddit, LinkedIn, and other forums provided a place for people to exchange ideas and refine tactics, creating a community for those navigating dual careers. Here, white-collar workers shared tips for managing the logistical and ethical complexities of holding down multiple roles. These virtual spaces became places to test and define the practice of overemployment, offering strategies for navigating an economic system that can often feel very one-sided.

In these communities, like-minded individuals found common ground, learning from each other's successes and setbacks. Influential voices emerged, distilling insights into practical advice and best practices, elevating overemployment from a series of isolated experiments to a defined strategy with its own set of norms and principles. These early adopters provided the framework and tools others needed to follow suit, transforming overemployment into a methodical approach to achieving financial security and independence.

The global pandemic helped to push the overemployment trend from the fringes into the mainstream. As remote work became standard, many realised they could potentially double or triple their income by holding down multiple roles —an option that simply wasn't viable in traditional, office-based employment. With companies adopting virtual operations, employees saw the chance to manage two or even three full-time roles simultaneously.

Overemployment quickly moved from an experiment to a viable income strategy. It's no longer just a financial hack; holding multiple full-time positions had become a strategic response to economic uncertainty, helping individuals reach financial goals more rapidly, or simply secure their financial future.

As traditional employment fragments further into contract-based or ad-hoc temporary roles, a growing community of overemployed workers is quietly redefining success in the modern workplace. Flying under the radar, spinning plates with several full time jobs on the boil at once, OEers have found a new job market niche that is increasingly raising the ire of employers who once demanded their full, undivided attention.

And while you might assume they're taking shortcuts, or cutting corners—at least doing a worse job than the average worker—the reality is more nuanced. To those on the outside, balancing multiple full-time roles may seem risky or even overwhelming. Yet for the overemployed, it's not about doing many jobs poorly, but optimising their time and efforts as a multiplier; it's about making the most of remote work's flexibility to pursue financial independence through intense bursts of focus. Juggling multiple jobs isn't for everyone, but for those who thrive within this framework, overemployment has become a calculated strategy—a way to navigate a shifting economy that rewards adaptability and resilience.

Each overemployed worker approaches this differently. Some coordinate jobs in separate time zones to manage their schedules, while others choose roles with fewer meetings to limit conflicts. What began as a way to maximise income has quickly evolved into a sophisticated strategy for achieving financial independence, with different schools of thought and philosophical underpinnings around best practices, ethics and accountability, and how to ensure you're never caught. For its adherents, the risks, ethical considerations, and challenges have come to define such a unique approach to work.

For many, the term "overemployment" might conjure images of non-stop work and constant hustle, but for those who practice it, it's a pragmatic approach to building multiple income streams in a world where financial security is never guaranteed. Each job ensures both wealth-building and stability, even in challenging times.

The overemployment movement is rooted in today's economic realities. While the pandemic accelerated the trend, remote work and economic pressures—rising living costs, wage stagnation, and debt—were already motivating people to seek additional income streams. Many participants in the overemployment community have seen how quickly jobs they depended on could disappear, a reality that has pushed them to take control of their financial futures.

This convergence of factors created the ideal environment for overemployment to take root and expand. What began as a survival tactic for some has become a source of personal and professional growth for others. The movement represents a shift in how people view work, blending flexibility with financial independence in a way that traditional employment models seldom allow. Overemployment isn't just a response to economic pressures but a proactive approach to navigating the modern economy, where adaptability and autonomy are increasingly valuable.

■■

In this book, we explore the day-to-day lives of overemployed workers, uncovering the systems they build to manage their roles, and keep their careers distinct, while staying within corporate and legal boundaries.

We meet some of the most experienced overemployed professionals to hear their stories, gathering insights and advice for those curious about managing multiple full-time jobs.

These chapters offer the rest of us 9-5 normies a window into a movement that is already helping to reshape lives, achieve career goals, and break through tax brackets.

CHAPTER 2

REIMAGINING WORK-LIFE BALANCE

Work-life balance once meant leaving the office at a reasonable hour, enjoying a long weekend here and there, or securing the elusive "remote Friday."

It was a modest aspiration, built on the principles of boundaries and predictability. But as overemployment gains ground, balance takes on a high-stakes redefinition. Instead of committing all one's time, loyalty, and performance to a single employer, the overemployed pursue a multi-layered livelihood, often balancing roles in different industries to secure multiple income streams.

For overemployed professionals, balance no longer means simply clocking out at a set time; it's the strategic calculus of managing meeting schedules, task loads, and personalities across separate reporting lines. In this landscape, "work-life balance" transforms into a delicate act of "work-life-work," a carefully stacked arrangement demanding precision and impeccable timing. Traditional employees juggle professional demands with personal obligations, but the overemployed add yet another full-time responsibility, making each day an exercise in balancing, prioritisation, and resourcefulness. However, the truth is that balance, for the overemployed, is rarely perfect. The goal is to keep each role—and life itself—just stable enough to sustain the charade.

Victor, a UX liaison, quickly learned that overemployment isn't just about multitasking; it's about triaging priorities at a granular level. His day begins with two early standups, meticulously timed to prevent overlap—a common theme. In his personal life, Victor has automated his daily routines— meal prep, bill pay, and other tasks—freeing up cognitive space for managing his dual roles. For him, every hour counts, and his day is optimised to prevent his jobs from clashing. When they do, he tends to just fall in a heap, so he aims to "sequencetask", as he's coined it, rather than multitask.

This relentless prioritisation extends beyond the workplace. Personal relationships, hobbies, and routines are restructured and condensed. For example, Victor schedules "deep work" sessions that cover him on both fronts, squeezes in gym visits at off-peak hours, and accepts social invitations sparingly, often using weekends to recharge. While there's no room for spontaneity, he finds the trade-off worthwhile for the financial stability it provides.

Success in this balancing act requires a unique mental agility—a resilience that makes overemployed workers adept at problem-solving and adjusting on the fly.

Tammy, a project manager, learned this firsthand when a client call was interrupted by a Slack message from her second boss at the worst possible moment. She now uses a colour-coded calendar system that flags high-risk times to minimise such conflicts. For her, each misstep is a learning opportunity, a data point in a continually refined strategy of overemployment.

Yet, living at this intensity has its pressures. Overemployed workers must constantly assess whether the long hours, tight schedules, and sacrifices align with the life they envisioned. For some, like Victor, the answer is a clear yes. For others, the mental toll can wear thin. But even on the hardest days, many find satisfaction in pulling off a lifestyle that defies conventional norms, demonstrating what's possible when every boundary is tested.

This unique work-life-work balance isn't sustainable for everyone, and the overemployed know it. Few imagine that they'll maintain dual roles indefinitely; the constant pressure can be exhausting. Yet, for now, the rewards outweigh the risks. Each day successfully balanced is an accomplishment, another step towards financial freedom and independence.

This recalibrated balance also extends to the personal realm. Overemployed professionals often keep their second job confidential, even from close friends, treating it as a guarded secret to maintain their lifestyle without raising suspicions. To them, this is not deception but self-protection—a strategy to sustain doubled income without doubling the risk of exposure.

Of course, the effort required to sustain this lifestyle can be exhausting. Managing two sets of deadlines, two networks of colleagues, and two streams of performance metrics demands creativity and meticulous planning. Yet the rewards are tangible and compelling: accelerated savings, early retirement, and lifestyle upgrades that a single job might never afford. For those who can make it work, overemployment isn't merely about adding hours—it's about doubling down on freedom and control, transcending traditional career paths.

This new take on work/life balance is a look into the future of all work, some in the community contest—what was once about wellbeing now a demanding game where the stakes are high, with agility and adaptability essential.

Overemployed workers have become masters of time management, skilled at multitasking without cracking under pressure. Their sights are set on a redefined success—one that blends financial ambition with an unprecedented level of personal control over both work and life. And in this balancing act, we glimpse a future where professional commitment means not loyalty to a single job, but to a sustainable, lucrative, and dynamic way of life.

CHAPTER 3

THE ART OF STRATEGIC DECEPTION

One might assume that working two full-time jobs means living in constant fear of discovery, sweating bullets at every unexpected Slack notification or unscheduled Zoom invite.

For the seasoned overemployment enjoyer, "strategic deception" is less about paranoia and more a high-level game of chess. It's about keeping calm under the scrutiny of not one but two sets of managers, sidestepping office politics, and curating an online presence that raises no flags. Welcome to a world where discretion, anonymity, and selective transparency are just as crucial as the work itself.

The dual job strategy requires a professional set of interchangeable masks to maintain multiple workplace personas with ease. Many overemployed workers craft separate identities, or at least highly curated versions of their personalities, tailored to each job. If the team at Job 1 knows you as a laid-back coder who loves a morning chat about Marvel movies, then at Job 2, perhaps you're a quiet night owl who prefers to dive straight into tasks, free from morning meetings. Keeping these characters distinct means you're not just balancing roles but embodying multiple avatars, all to maintain the illusion that each company has your undivided attention.

Much of this art hinges on managing presence—or, perhaps more accurately, managing absence. For instance, the overemployed are careful about staying "available" on work messaging platforms without being conspicuously present. In the virtual office of one job, they're expertly crafting an email response while at the other, they might be juggling a video call. Few understand this tightrope as well as the overemployed, who spend their days toggling between Slack windows, calendar invites, and deadlines, all with an expert's flair for evasion.

Tools and technology become lifelines, too. Many develop sophisticated methods of keeping tasks compartmentalised —using browser profiles, multiple devices, automated scripts, and workflow organisers. Some even automate parts of their workload, using scripts to handle routine tasks like data entry, updates, or meeting scheduling—freeing themselves up to be in two virtual places at once. These are not passive actors; they are actively engaged in a complex dance of work, constantly fine-tuning their systems to ensure their ruse holds firm. But as any master of deception knows, even the most meticulous plan must sometimes flex. Overemployed workers understand that things don't always go to plan, and they're adept at rolling with the punches, ready to downplay suspicions or excuse a missed notification with disarming charm and a well-timed apology.

While the overemployed see strategic deception as a form of art, a necessary skill in the portfolio of modern work, they also acknowledge its risks. Get too bold, and the façade crumbles; get too careful, and the effort starts to outweigh the gain.

It's another thread of the balancing act—one that demands constant awareness, flawless execution, and an unwavering focus on the ultimate goal. For those who can pull it off, the payoff isn't just financial. It's a triumph of agency, a satisfaction in outsmarting a system designed to hold them to one job, one paycheck, one employer-approved view of "commitment." The result? A career that feels almost cinematic in its intrigue, and a lifestyle that redefines the boundaries of modern work.

CHAPTER 4

THE PERFECT DOUBLE LIFE

For most who engage in it, overemployment is more than a "get rich quick" scheme. It's a practical response to financial pressures and a way to protect oneself against the unpredictability of the corporate world.

As a lifestyle choice, overemployment isn't only about juggling tasks—it's a broader, more meta mindset that requires building two entirely separate existences, each with its own rhythms, personalities, and quirks. To a manager at Company X, you're a strategic thinker who prefers asynchronous communication; to the team at Company Y, you're a data-driven doer, always on call for a quick chat. This double life is a high-stakes exercise in compartmentalisation, where each job feeds its own narrative, and each identity exists in a distinct silo, hermetically sealed from the other.

The foundation of this double life is *structure*—a meticulously crafted division of time, tasks, and emotional energy with an overarching vision of how that's all accomplished. Here, calendars become blueprints, colour-coded and synchronised, with blocks for "deep work" masking times when the other job calls for attention. Both worlds keep humming along without colliding. For many, this set-up goes beyond mere utility. It's an art form, a personal ecosystem designed to streamline their own unique version of double duty.

But perhaps the greatest feat is managing communication. Every call, email, and chat is a calculated move in a chess game, where the slightest misstep—a moment of hesitation, a lagging webcam—can arouse suspicion. To navigate these waters, the overemployed adopt rules for engagement as rigid as a military code: cameras off whenever possible, scripted responses that work across contexts, and a masterful command of the mute button. Even greetings get tailored. To one team, it's a casual "Hey all!" and to the other, a crisp "Good morning." Over time, these become muscle memory, subconscious signals that activate the appropriate identity on cue.

One might think that these two lives would breed guilt or paranoia, but for the overemployed, they are simply parallel pathways to achieving a goal. The question isn't about whether they're "cheating the system"—it's about maximising the hand they've been dealt. These dual identities are badges of resourcefulness, symbols of a new professionalism that values results over face time and output over hours logged. Taken no more seriously than an online gaming character, an avatar account that they can jump in and out of easily. Only here it's their professional persona with their real name and address, and elements of their real personality peppered through for believability. Each role bolsters the other, financially and mentally, creating a level of security that traditional employment models can't match.

Of course, the double life isn't without its risks, and the overemployed know it. Mistakes can happen: the errant email sent to the wrong inbox, the mixed-up meeting invite, the occasional slip in tone that reveals a fracture in the historical narrative.

CHAPTER 5

CALCULATED PRESENCE

For the overemployed, the "routine" workday is anything but. Rather, it's a high-focus ballet of Zoom links, time zones, and well-placed calendar blocks. There's nothing haphazard about it; every moment, from the quiet minutes before the first login to the winding down of a second or third meeting, is calculated. And each day is punctuated with tiny gambles—a string of small, controlled risks that collectively weave a lifestyle built on both precision and freedom.

Sophia is a game designer juggling a daring triple life. By day—and sometimes long into the night—she works as a senior level designer for two AAA game studios while secretly building her own indie startup. Her home office is an intricate setup designed for rapid toggling: three monitors, isolated workflows, and carefully segregated accounts for Slack, Discord, and email. To the untrained eye, it's a typical creative workspace, adorned with concept sketches and reference books. But with a swipe of her trackpad, Sophia seamlessly switches between companies, diving into each project as though it's her sole focus.

An early stand-up for her first studio at 9:00 a.m.? No problem—she shifts her indie team's morning sprint review to 10:00 a.m., leaving a narrow gap to dive into brainstorming with her second studio. The timing is precise, a high-stakes game of professional leapfrog that requires flawless execution. Her system is smooth, almost mechanical—until the inevitable ping of an unexpected notification reminds her that chaos is always one misstep away.

For Sophia, the ever-present risk isn't just a threat; it's fuel. Balancing three creative worlds sharpens her instincts, forcing her into a state of constant readiness. This heightened focus is more than survival; it's her competitive edge. Over time, she's honed the art of strategic excellence: knowing exactly when to impress and when to fade into the background. At Studio A, she excels in group calls, knowing her creative director prizes collaboration over speed. At Studio B, she delivers impeccable builds ahead of schedule, aware that metrics matter more than face time. Meanwhile, her startup thrives in the cracks between, with her team trained to thrive independently while she provides guidance in bursts.

By tailoring her presence to each context, Sophia embodies the perfect employee for all three ventures—a master of selective engagement, showing her best side where it matters most. Her triple life is a feat of creative choreography, and while every day feels like a high-wire act, it's also where she thrives.

But for all its poise, this lifestyle comes with a baseline of anxiety. The overemployed know that their setup is, by nature, fragile; a single careless email or calendar misstep could unravel weeks or months of effort. They operate in a realm where improvisation meets precision, where every interaction is a calculated risk. Still, as each day ticks by without discovery, they grow more resilient, more emboldened.

In this calculated chaos, overemployment is no longer just a money-making tactic; it becomes an exercise in skill mastery, a mental discipline that strengthens with each workday pulled off without a hitch.

The overemployed don't merely "show up" to work; they curate their presence with surgical precision, understanding that in the digital office, presence *is* perception. To managers Nora appears as engaged as any colleague—just as vocal on Slack, equally reliable in responding to email, and ever-present at critical meetings. But beneath this professional veneer lies a carefully orchestrated deception, a balancing act designed to fulfil two roles without compromising either. And for the overemployed, this is where the real work begins.

Ethan has nailed down an "availability window" that spans from 9 a.m. to 7 p.m., allowing him to blend two separate 9-to-5s into a ten-hour block that straddles two time zones. His mornings are reserved for Company A, a tech startup in San Francisco that thrives on early standups and brainstorming sessions. Afternoons? Company B, a healthcare firm on the East Coast where expectations lean toward asynchronous communication and pre-recorded project updates. Each day, Ethan sets his Slack status to "In a meeting" for Company A when he's on a call for Company B—and vice versa. No one questions his engagement; in fact, both companies praise his "flexibility" and "commitment." But the magic behind his reputation is really just a well-rehearsed charade.

Ethan's story isn't unique among the overemployed. For many, the most nerve-wracking part of the job is navigating video calls. Here, presence isn't just an icon or a green bubble on a messaging app; it's a performance where every raised eyebrow, every nod, even the backdrop of their virtual surroundings is scrutinised. These are the subtleties that could raise a manager's suspicions. To avoid this, seasoned overemployed professionals often set up separate workspaces or at least switch up the details—a quick change of shirt, a slight adjustment in lighting, maybe a family photo swapped out for a bookshelf in the background.

This balancing act of digital presence isn't just a minor inconvenience; it becomes an art form, demanding not only attention to detail but a mental stamina few careers require. It's cognitively taxing, even exhausting, to monitor how one is perceived across two distinct roles. Yet, for the overemployed, it's a necessary discipline. A core skill in their unique repertoire. And each successful day only emboldens them, not because they're fooling anyone, but because they're proving that traditional constraints on work —geography, schedules, visibility—are, in fact, negotiable. The double life they lead isn't a betrayal of commitment but

Rob Hackney

a testament to adaptability in a world that, until now, has been slow to adapt to them.

CHAPTER 6

SUCCESS IN THE JOB MARKETPLACE

The overemployed approach the job market with a precision most career coaches would envy. For them, every application, every interview, every offer is a calculated move in a larger game of career chess. They don't have lines in the water; they cast a net. Unlike the single-job seeker, they're not just looking for a good fit—they're hunting for roles that balance, complement, and enhance the ones they already have. It's not just about finding a job; it's about constructing a puzzle where every piece slots seamlessly into a life of dual (or even triple) employment.

The job description is their first test. On the surface, it may promise an exciting opportunity, but the overemployed have learned to look beyond the buzzwords. They've become experts in decoding the euphemisms of corporate speak: "dynamic environment" might mean chaos; "wear many hats" is often shorthand for overwork; and "high visibility role" usually translates to constant scrutiny. Instead, they seek out signals of autonomy—terms like "results-oriented," "self-starter," and the ever-reliable "asynchronous work." These are the hidden cues that suggest a job could quietly slot into the rhythm of an overemployed schedule.

This search extends beyond the job posting itself. The overemployed are relentless researchers, diving into Glassdoor reviews and LinkedIn threads to parse the reality behind a company's promises. They read between the lines of employee feedback, hunting for mentions of flexible managers, independent workflows, and cultures that prioritise outcomes over micromanagement. Every scrap of intel feeds into their decision-making.

When the interviews begin, their game shifts. For most candidates, interviews are about selling themselves; for the overemployed, they're also about interrogating the company. Each question they ask is designed to unearth the realities of the role. Phrases like "What does a typical week look like?" or "How do you measure success in this position?" aren't casual inquiries—they're deliberate probes, designed to gauge workload, timelines, and managerial expectations. The goal isn't just to land the job but to ensure it's a manageable addition to their already intricate schedule.

And then there's the matter of presence. Overemployed candidates are masters of first impressions. They show up to interviews polished, professional, and prepared, projecting an air of dependable competence. They know these first encounters are critical, not just for landing the role but for setting the tone for the future—one where trust and autonomy are implicit.

Once the offer is secured, the onboarding phase begins, and with it, the challenge of integrating into a new team without missing a beat in their existing roles. This is where the overemployed truly shine, leveraging their adaptability and experience to embed themselves seamlessly. The first few weeks are crucial. They overperform strategically, delivering on deadlines and participating actively in meetings, creating a reputation as someone who can be relied upon without question. But even in these moments of high visibility, they're setting boundaries—subtle, almost imperceptible limits that ensure their availability doesn't spiral into unsustainable demands.

Technology becomes a silent partner in this process. From browser profiles to workflow automation, the overemployed lean on tools to compartmentalise their job seeking, business as usual tasks, and streamline efforts. They automate repetitive processes, offloading mundane tasks to free up cognitive bandwidth. Their digital workspaces are temples of organisation, designed to keep the chaos of multiple jobs from spilling into one another.

But the real art of onboarding lies in how they navigate relationships. Building just enough rapport with colleagues and managers to foster goodwill, without becoming so visible that they attract unnecessary attention, is a delicate balance. It's a social tightrope: be warm, be competent, but don't overshare or over-invest. The overemployed know that the less they're noticed, the freer they are to operate.

And still, the market beckons. Even while fully employed— sometimes doubly so—they're scanning for the next opportunity, the next puzzle piece. The overemployed are perpetual job seekers, always with one eye on the horizon. Their commitment isn't to any one employer but to the lifestyle they've built, a career that bends to their ambitions rather than the other way around.

It's this constant recalibration that defines their success. When a job becomes too demanding or no longer aligns, they pivot. When a better offer arises, they shift. Each role is evaluated not just for its pay or title but for how it fits into the grander scheme. Every move is deliberate, every choice a step toward greater autonomy, financial security, and control.

For the overemployed, the job market isn't just a place to find work. It's a proving ground, a battlefield, a theatre of opportunity. And in this game, they're not just participants—they're the architects, designing careers that defy convention and rewriting the rules of what work can be.

With this mindset, success isn't a monolithic achievement. It's not a gold watch after decades of service to one company or even the celebration of climbing one clearly defined corporate ladder. Instead, it's a mosaic—composed of freedom, financial security, professional growth, and the quiet satisfaction of outmanoeuvring a system that demands unwavering loyalty while offering little in return.

Katie is a UX designer who began her overemployment journey out of necessity. Her first job, while creatively fulfilling, was at a boutique agency with an uninspiring salary. So, she added a second role—a remote gig at a tech company. What started as a short-term solution to her financial woes turned into a stepping stone for an entirely new career trajectory. By leveraging the projects and skills from both jobs, Katie built an impressive portfolio faster than either role alone could have allowed. In a matter of two years, she transitioned from being a mid-level designer to landing a six-figure lead position at a multinational corporation, her experience and skills bolstered by a dual-role strategy.

Katie's story reflects one of the most compelling benefits of overemployment: *compressed career growth*. By participating in two professional ecosystems simultaneously, she accelerated her exposure to diverse workflows, toolsets, and corporate cultures. The variety enriched her skills and demonstrated her value to future employers, who saw her versatility without needing to know the full story.

Financial freedom is often the first marker of success for the overemployed. After all, dual incomes open doors—paying off debt, investing in property, saving for early retirement. But the impact often extends beyond the monetary. For some, like Kevin, a data scientist juggling two full-time jobs, the real victory lies in reclaiming control over his time.

Kevin's first job demanded gruelling hours with little payoff. By taking on a second, Kevin found he could strategically redistribute his effort. Both jobs received only his *best effort in the moments that mattered most*. No longer reliant on one company for his livelihood, he negotiated down his hours at Job A, shifted more of his focus to Job B, and carved out time for personal projects that had languished for years. Success for Kevin wasn't just a fatter bank account; it was the ability to take charge of his own narrative—professional, financial, and personal.

For others, overemployment becomes a tool for diversification. Entrepreneurs like Janelle have used their dual incomes to bootstrap passion projects. A cybersecurity consultant by day and an online-course creator by night, Janelle built her education platform with the stability of two incomes, turning her side hustle into a fully-fledged business within three years. Overemployment didn't just supplement her earnings; it catalysed her dream of independence.

Success isn't just about individual achievement; it's also about the broader lessons overemployment teaches. The ability to adapt, pivot, and thrive in ambiguity—qualities once reserved for the C-suite—become second nature to the overemployed. These aren't just survival skills; they're marketable skills.

Raj, a mid-level project manager, once felt stuck in his role at a global logistics firm. His first overemployment opportunity was a temporary contract in the same field. Balancing the two roles forced Raj to master the art of prioritisation. He became adept at managing competing timelines, communicating effectively with diverse teams, and using data-driven tools to track productivity. When a leadership position opened at Job 1, Raj applied—and got it.

In interviews, he framed his ability to juggle priorities as proof of his readiness for higher-stakes responsibilities. The hiring panel agreed, none the wiser about the context in which he'd honed these skills. For Raj, overemployment wasn't just a secret; it was his training ground for the next phase of his career.

Sometimes, overemployment yields unlikely allies. Amelia, a marketing strategist, was accidentally discovered by a manager who caught a glimpse of her second role during a Zoom call. She braced for the fallout—but instead, her manager surprised her. Intrigued rather than angered, they asked Amelia how she managed to balance her work so effectively.

By the end of their conversation, the manager had extracted a playbook of strategies that would later inform the company's approach to hybrid work. Amelia's success became a case study for productivity rather than a cause for termination. Stories like Amelia's are rare but not unheard of, a testament to the fact that even the rigid boundaries of corporate life are starting to bend under the weight of new ways of working.

For all its challenges, overemployment offers a glimpse of what the future of work might hold. As traditional job structures erode and workers prioritise autonomy, those who master this lifestyle become pioneers in a new labour market paradigm. They're rewriting the rules—showing that success isn't just about climbing one ladder but about navigating multiple paths.

Rob Hackney

The careers of the overemployed are a testament to resilience, ingenuity, and the human desire for more—more growth, more freedom, more agency. Their stories remind us that success doesn't come from playing by the rules. It comes from redefining them.

CHAPTER 7

OVEREMPLOYEE'S TOOLBOX

The email arrived on a Tuesday morning: *Fw: Mandatory all-hands meeting to discuss our updated employment policies.*

Sasha's stomach dropped as she scanned the message from her new employer's HR department. After years of carefully balancing multiple remote positions, she knew these policy updates often spelled trouble for the overemployed. The modern corporate landscape had become increasingly vigilant about employees holding multiple jobs, with many companies implementing strict anti-moonlighting policies backed by serious consequences —from immediate termination to the threat of withheld pay.

The reality of overemployment isn't found in the dramatic moments of near-discovery or close calls, though these certainly exist. Instead, it lives in the mundane details of daily management, in the careful orchestration of multiple professional lives that must never intersect. Success in this world demands more than just time management skills or technical prowess—it requires a fundamental understanding of corporate dynamics and human psychology. The first rule of overemployment is, perhaps unsurprisingly, absolute discretion.

In the OE community, this maxim is treated as gospel. Even trusted friends and family members are often kept in the dark, with many practitioners sharing their situation only with spouses or accountants. This secrecy extends beyond simple verbal discretion—it encompasses every aspect of one's professional presence, from carefully curated LinkedIn profiles to meticulously managed digital footprints. It is the base layer on which all other elements of the overemployment toolbox are built.

The technical aspects of maintaining multiple jobs have evolved into something of an art form. Veteran OEers emphasise the importance of digital hygiene: separate devices for separate jobs when possible, careful attention to which microphone is active during calls, and the strategic use of "frozen" or hibernated professional networks to prevent accidental cross-pollination between roles. These aren't just paranoid precautions—they're essential safeguards against the kind of small mistakes that can unravel even the most carefully constructed OE arrangement.

"The key to successful OE isn't finding the perfect jobs," explains Marcus, a software developer who has maintained multiple positions for over two years. "It's about finding jobs that complement each other in terms of meeting schedules, reporting structures, and work intensity." The ideal scenario often involves larger companies with multiple layers of management, where individual contributors can maintain more autonomy and face less direct oversight. When searching for additional positions, experienced practitioners often submit hundreds of applications, carefully screening potential opportunities for compatibility with their existing commitments.

The management of expectations becomes crucial once multiple positions are secured. The goal isn't to be the superstar employee in any single role, but rather to maintain consistent, reliable performance across all positions. This often means deliberately avoiding the appearance of being a workaholic—a counterintuitive strategy that actually helps prevent the kind of increased responsibilities that can derail an overemployment arrangement.

Meeting management emerges as one of the most critical skills in the toolkit. Successful practitioners develop a repertoire of strategies for handling conflicting schedules. Unpredictable cadence of camera participation in video calls helps maintain the appearance of engagement while providing flexibility. Simple requests to reschedule meetings—"Can we move the 1pm to 2pm to avoid a clash?"—often go unquestioned when used sparingly and without elaborate explanations.

The physical setup of one's workspace plays a crucial role in successful OE management. Multiple monitors, keyboard/mouse setups that can quickly switch between systems, and sufficient desk space aren't luxuries—they're necessities.

When overlapping meetings become unavoidable, prioritising group sessions where others carry the conversational load over one-on-one interactions can help manage the chaos.

But perhaps the most under-appreciated aspect of successful overemployment is the maintenance of physical and mental health. The demands of managing multiple positions can quickly lead to burnout without proper boundaries and self-care routines. Early morning exercise, consistent sleep schedules, and proper nutrition aren't just wellness buzzwords—they're essential components of a sustainable OE lifestyle.

The question of additional duties and scope creep requires particular attention in an OE context. When one employer begins adding responsibilities beyond the original job description, the careful balance of multiple roles can quickly become untenable. Successful OE practitioners become masters of the strategic pushback, learning to maintain boundaries without appearing uncooperative.

"Documentation becomes your best friend," shares Lisa, a project manager who has navigated multiple roles for years. "Having a clear record of your original job description and duties provides crucial leverage when pushing back against scope creep." The art lies in maintaining professional relationships while firmly protecting your time and energy—resources that, in an OE arrangement, are already carefully allocated across multiple commitments.

The rising tide of automation and artificial intelligence tools has become a crucial ally for the overemployed community. While these tools can't replace human judgment or interaction, they can dramatically streamline routine tasks and help maintain the appearance of constant availability. Email sorting bots, automated status updates, and sophisticated calendar management systems create a foundation of efficiency that makes multiple jobs manageable.

Yet the use of automation comes with its own risks. Every automated system requires careful monitoring and occasional adjustment to prevent the kind of errors that can expose an OE arrangement. The goal isn't to automate everything possible, but rather to strategically apply automation to tasks where the benefits outweigh the potential risks.

The ethical considerations of overemployment cannot be ignored. Critics argue that it constitutes a form of deception, while practitioners counter that they're responding rationally to an economic system that offers decreasing job security and stagnant wages. The reality lies somewhere in between, with many OE practitioners actually delivering higher quality work due to their refined efficiency and time management skills.

As corporate awareness of overemployment grows, so too do the challenges of maintaining multiple positions. Yet the fundamental forces driving professionals toward OE—economic uncertainty, the desire for financial independence, and the increasing feasibility of remote work —show no signs of abating. Success in this world requires a delicate balance of technical skill, emotional intelligence, and strategic thinking.

For anyone who is overemployed, automation isn't just a convenience—it's a lifeline. Balancing two or more full-time jobs requires a level of efficiency that no ordinary workflow can achieve alone. This is where automation comes in, transforming repetitive tasks, filling in the gaps, and buying precious minutes from the constant demands of multiple roles. Automation is the unsung hero of overemployment, allowing its practitioners to achieve the impossible: doing two days' worth of work in a single day, and doing it so well that neither employer suspects a thing.

Meet Paul, a business analyst turned automation expert whose first overemployment experience quickly spiralled from a casual experiment into a double career fuelled by productivity hacks. For Paul, success in overemployment relies on his suite of tools: bots to handle menial tasks, scripts to update documents, and complex workflows that keep his deliverables on autopilot. He's built a network of automated systems that operate in the background, silently managing the small but time-consuming tasks that once took up his day. From email sorting bots to Slack status updaters, Paul's automation arsenal makes his double life possible and keeps him ahead of deadlines he might otherwise miss.

One of Paul's most ingenious creations is his task-routing bot—an AI script that monitors both his inboxes for job-specific keywords, prioritising the emails that need immediate attention while routing low-priority tasks to scheduled blocks throughout his week. The bot even responds to emails with pre-drafted responses, algorithmically mixing up the wording occasionally to help him maintain the appearance of a diligent and attentive employee. While his colleagues marvel at his "quick response time," Paul sits back, knowing his bot is handling the bulk of his inbox while he focuses on more critical tasks for both jobs.

And Paul's approach goes beyond email. Using browser automation tools, he's created shortcuts to navigate the necessary internal systems for each role without manual input. For instance, he has macros set up to pull and update key data in a matter of seconds, effectively allowing him to submit end-of-day reports, manage performance metrics, and keep an eye on deadlines without lifting a finger. It's a machine-driven symphony, where each system plays its part to maintain the appearance of productivity at an inhuman speed. As agent LLMs with bespoke RAG training have come online in recent years, Paul has been elevated from a lowly member of the string section to now conduct the whole orchestra. For Paul, the success of his dual career isn't just about balancing two workloads; it's about mastering the technology that lets him do both with a level of efficiency his single-job counterparts rarely need.

But automation has its risks. Paul learned this the hard way after an early incident when his email bot, misinterpreting a keyword, responded to his manager with a form response intended for a client. Luckily, he caught the mistake before any real harm was done, but the incident served as a stark reminder: automation is a tool, not a foolproof solution. And for the overemployed, it's essential to keep a vigilant eye on every automated system—optimising, adjusting, testing, and occasionally overriding when things get too close for comfort.

Over time, the overemployed community has collectively developed an arsenal of tools, strategies, and best practices for automation. From using Trello boards to track task deadlines across roles to utilising Notion and its inbuilt AI for quick project iteration. These tools create a seamless work environment where roles blend effortlessly, each task finding its place in an overall workflow that's both cohesive and compartmentalised. Many rely on IFTTT (If This Then That) tooling, or integration hubs such as Zapier to trigger actions across applications—an email received in one inbox might automatically trigger a calendar update, or a task created in Slack may auto-populate a task manager. The goal? To minimise the number of times they need to manually handle these trivial but necessary steps, freeing them to focus on tasks that actually require their expertise. Less touches at scale means more bandwidth for the tasks that require human attention.

Even the management of their own visibility is often automated. For eg, some might use Slack status automation to shuffle availability status, managing competing demands while automation obfuscates on their behalf. Automation becomes as much a shield as a productivity tool—it provides a cover, a tactical invisibility that ensures both roles are maintained without risking burnout or discovery.

Yet, despite its many benefits, automation can feel like a double-edged sword. For some, the constant vigilance required to monitor scripts, manage bots, and troubleshoot automation errors adds a layer of complexity that can be as demanding as the work itself. Automation frees up time but also demands a sharpness, a constant awareness of the systems in play and an ability to troubleshoot on the fly. The overemployed live in a constant state of readiness, knowing that while automation can make the impossible possible, it also means that even the smallest oversight can have outsized consequences.

For Paul, and for many in the overemployed community, this dedication to automating their work lives is an empowering choice. It's a quiet protest against the inefficiencies of traditional employment, a way to sidestep mindless tasks and focus on what truly matters. Many have been more forthcoming with such solutions, only to be fired once the company became aware that a script could perform the majority of a worker's processes. While it may seem selfish or deceptive to perform work this way, keeping it quiet is the only strategic path to longevity, and ultimately the work is completed on time and to spec.

For those who can pull it off, automation is more than just a timesaver; it's a passport to a new kind of freedom, a life where multiple careers coexist—not because of superhuman effort, but because technology, when wielded correctly, makes the unthinkable achievable.

The path of overemployment isn't for everyone. It demands constant vigilance, impeccable organisation, and the ability to maintain multiple professional personas without losing one's authentic self in the process. Yet for those who can master its complexities, it offers a level of financial security and professional autonomy that traditional employment rarely provides. In a world where job security increasingly feels like an outdated concept, the ability to maintain multiple income streams while delivering value to multiple employers may well become the new normal for ambitious professionals willing to walk this challenging path.

CHAPTER 8

NAVIGATING THE SOCIAL MINEFIELD

In a world that thrives on noise, the overemployed have discovered an unlikely superpower: silence. It's not just a survival skill—it's a form of control. When your life is built on the careful balancing act of two (or more) careers, every word has weight. Silence is not the absence of communication but the presence of discipline.

Lara is a senior project manager juggling dual tech roles. For her, silence is a deliberate act of self-preservation. "People love to talk," she says. "It's easier not to give them ammunition." She calls it her "vow of omission"—a commitment to withholding details that might expose her secret life. To her colleagues at Job 1, she's simply "too busy" for happy hour; with her family, she shifts the conversation to hobbies or Netflix recommendations. It's not deceit—it's precision.

But silence isn't merely defensive. Lara wields it to deflect curiosity and maintain control of her narrative. The less she reveals, the less there is for anyone to question. The less traction she allows anyone to get on her as a legitimate human behind the mask, the less attack surfaces she exposes. In an era where oversharing is encouraged, her restraint is almost radical. It allows her to exist in multiple realities without colliding with herself.

This practice, however, comes with emotional side effects. Silence can be isolating. Conversations that once felt effortless—lunch breaks with colleagues, casual banter at family gatherings—become fraught with potential hazards. Lara finds herself holding back, even when there's no real threat, just out of habit. She describes it as living in "self-imposed ambiguity." And yet, the alternative—openness—feels unthinkable.

Ironically, for someone so committed to secrecy, Lara has found an unexpected sense of community in the anonymous world of online forums. In these virtual spaces, silence is broken without consequence. Here, she and others like her swap tips on managing overlapping meetings, laugh about close calls, and share the weight of their unconventional lifestyles. "It's the only place I feel seen," she admits. The forums have become a sanctuary—a reminder that she's not alone in this carefully curated silence.

Silence isn't about withholding for its own sake. It's about boundaries. It's about knowing what's yours to keep and what the world doesn't need to know. For Lara and countless others, silence is not a void but a carefully constructed filter. It's not easy, and it's not without cost—but for those walking the tightrope, it's indispensable.

Silence may shield the overemployed socially, but it's not the whole strategy. In a world where every interaction—every Slack thread, LinkedIn post, and Zoom icebreaker—can ripple out into unintended exposure, the overemployed need more than restraint. They need agility. Emotional IQ. A radar for drama. Social interactions are the ultimate high-stakes game that requires finesse, intuition, and a constant recalibration of boundaries.

The workplace isn't the only minefield. Personal relationships also demand careful navigation. Kiera, a software developer with two high-pressure jobs, has taken the principle of selective disclosure to heart. Her husband knows she works two jobs but doesn't know the specifics. "Not because I don't trust him," she says, "but because the less he knows, the less he can potentially blurt out." Family gatherings have become a tightrope walk of vague answers and artful deflections. "It's exhausting," Kiera admits, "but it's necessary."

For the overemployed, even casual social norms like LinkedIn updates can become existential dilemmas. Updating one profile risks drawing attention to the other; not updating at all risks raising suspicion among colleagues. The solution? Mastery of the pivot. The overemployed become adept at steering conversations back to safe topics: the weather, shared hobbies, or universal frustrations like traffic and taxes. They learn to listen more than they speak, letting others fill the silences they leave behind.

Kiera likens it to a dynamic business skillset: the ability to read a room, adapt on the fly, and maintain composure under scrutiny. "It's exhausting, but it's also empowering," she says. "You realise how much control you have when you stop giving everything away."

CHAPTER 9

THE ILLUSION OF TRANSPARENCY

Transparency in the workplace has become a buzzword, with companies preaching "authenticity" and "open communication" as the building blocks of a healthy work culture. But for the overemployed, transparency is an illusion—something they build without ever fully buying into. Their version of "being open" is calibrated, strategically orchestrated, and often more convincing than genuine transparency. They know that appearing transparent, while actually concealing half of their professional life, is a nuanced dance that requires tact, foresight, and occasionally, bold creativity.

One of the most masterful practitioners of this illusion is Dani, an account manager who thrives in the open office culture of both her roles. To her colleagues at Job 1, she's forthcoming about her calendar conflicts, claiming that "client calls" often pull her away from internal meetings. At Job 2, she's developed a reputation for being highly focused and "in the zone," especially when she has blocked hours for "project work" that conveniently overlap with her peak hours at Job 1. It requires both consistency and adaptation; she's transparent enough to keep everyone at ease but elusive enough to protect her dual commitments. Her strategy is not to over-explain, but to allow small insights—enough to craft a plausible professional identity—while never offering up the full picture.

But there's a risk that comes with this illusion. Dani understands that the more details she shares, the more questions she invites, so her transparency remains at surface level. She knows exactly which meetings require a vocal contribution and which ones she can drift through, her camera off, her microphone muted. On particularly busy days, she relies on well-timed messages to telegraph presence: a Slack post during a company meeting, a friendly emoji in the chat, a perfectly placed "Great point!" in response to someone else's comment. It's all part of a careful choreography that ensures no one ever doubts her attention or loyalty.

And then there's the matter of visibility. As a rule, the overemployed avoid LinkedIn updates or posts that might tip off connections about their dual roles. If they need to maintain a LinkedIn presence, they'll carefully control it—leaving job titles vague, omitting overlapping dates, or sharing posts with anodyne insights that raise no flags. Dani goes so far as to list herself as a "consultant" in both roles on her profile, keeping her network connections for each job strictly separated. It's a cloak-and-dagger approach to professional networking that allows her to navigate social media while keeping her dual life hidden in plain sight.

But there's an unexpected benefit here, too. By carefully cultivating an illusion of transparency, the overemployed become adept at managing the complexities of remote work culture. They know which communications get noticed and which can slide under the radar; they understand when visibility matters and when to keep skimming by across the surface, under the radar. This skill, while born of necessity, often makes them more efficient, more productive, and, ironically, more trustworthy in the eyes of their employers. The very discipline required to maintain the illusion also sharpens their focus, adding a layer of conscientiousness that many find missing in their peers who are tied to a single role.

This crafted transparency is far from superficial; it's a core skill for the overemployed, one they practice with the precision of a stage performer. And like all well-received method acting performances, the beauty lies in its subtlety. When done right, no one suspects a thing. To both of her employers, Dani appears as a model of transparency—open, reliable, and always present, a professional whose integrity is as unquestionable as her work ethic. And in that carefully constructed image, she finds a strange sense of satisfaction. Not because she's hiding the truth, but because she's mastered the art of selective honesty, transforming the idea of transparency into something far more complex, and, ultimately, more powerful.

CHAPTER 10

THE BURNOUT PARADOX

For those who partake in overemployment, burnout isn't just a risk—it's practically a given. Yet, oddly enough, many of the overemployed report feeling more energised by their work than they did with a single, traditional role. It's a paradox that runs through the core of overemployment: the more work they take on, the sharper their focus, the more deliberate their time management, and the greater the sense of personal control. The risk of burnout is ever-present, but so, too, is the allure of empowerment, the drive to outsmart the system and reach financial goals at an accelerated pace.

Jamie, a financial analyst, after years of climbing the corporate ladder, had reached a plateau. The pay raises had levelled off, and promotions were promised with caveats. But since stepping into the world of overemployment, Jamie has become more productive, regimented, and—paradoxically—fulfilled. His two jobs require an almost superhuman level of focus, and yet, for the first time in years, he's feeling stimulated. One role pulls him into complex market analysis, while the other focuses on product development finance. These aren't fields most people would take on lightly, but for Jamie, the mental challenge and the financial boost make the occasional fatigue feel like a fair trade.

This paradox is rooted in the freedom overemployment offers. With a clear financial endgame, most overemployed individuals aren't working two jobs indefinitely. Instead, they're setting concrete goals—whether it's building an investment portfolio, paying down debts, or creating a fund for early retirement. By choosing their own finish line, they redefine the terms of burnout. In a conventional role, burnout often arises from the sense of being trapped, a cycle of responsibilities without a clear endpoint. The constant fear that if we push back too hard, the rug will be quickly pulled. But for the overemployed, there's always a light at the end of the tunnel, a financial benchmark they're aiming for that will let them eventually step back. An ease of navigation that stems from knowing they have more irons in the fire if Plan A fails to unfurl as intended.

Yet, there's no doubt that some days are brutal. Claire, who juggles two project management roles, recalls how one particularly intense week saw her jumping between back-to-back meetings for 14 hours straight, one calendar invite blending into the next. That Friday, as she closed her laptop, the exhaustion was so profound she questioned her entire approach. She was close to hitting her savings target, she reminded herself, but it had taken a toll on her sleep, her health, and her relationships. Burnout, she realised, was a reality she had to manage as carefully as her work hours.

Many OEers have developed techniques to stave off burnout. They schedule micro-breaks, take short walks, adopt "digital detox" weekends, monitor blue light exposure, and rigorously protect their sleep. Unlike conventional workers who may feel guilty about a quick break, the overemployed see these moments of rest as essential, not optional. Their strategy isn't about escaping work; it's about maintaining a high level of output without sacrificing the clarity that keeps their dual roles manageable.

In the end, the burnout paradox is more than just another part of the work/life balancing act to moderate exhaustion and empowerment. Quite the opposite.

For those who thrive in overemployment, it becomes a mental training ground, a test of endurance, and a calculated push toward a self-defined goal. It's ankle weights for the mind. A powerful redefinition of work stress, self-worth, and mental fortitude, driven by a calculated decision to take control of one's time, earning potential, and career trajectory.

CHAPTER 11

THE FINANCIAL FAST TRACK

Michael's spreadsheet told a story that would seem impossible to most: seven separate payroll deposits, totalling just over $83,000, had landed in his various bank accounts that month. Five years ago, he'd been a mid-level software architect making $130,000 a year. Now, at thirty-four, he was on track to clear $1.2 million in annual compensation—all while working remotely from a quiet suburb in Colorado. But the truly remarkable part wasn't the money itself. It was how Michael, like a growing number of extreme overemployment practitioners, was systematically transforming these multiple income streams into a foundation for permanent financial independence.

"The first million is defence," Michael explains, referencing a mantra common among the upper echelons of the OE community. "Everything after that is offence." His strategy, refined through years of managing multiple technical roles, had evolved far beyond simply collecting paychecks. Each new position was evaluated not just for its immediate compensation, but for its potential to provide deeper technical expertise, industry connections, or insights that could be leveraged into future opportunities.

The world of extreme overemployment—those managing five or more concurrent positions—operates on a different plane than typical OE practitioners. These aren't just professionals supplementing their income with an extra job or two. They're sophisticated operators who have turned job-stacking into a high-stakes financial strategy, often earning seven figures annually while building substantial investment portfolios and launching their own ventures.

James, a former front end engineer who managed to juggle five, six, and then seven senior positions across different time zones, reached his all-time career peak salary at USD$1.8 million in annual compensation. His approach was methodical: each role was selected based on its timezone, asynchronous reporting, and a very narrow tech stack that he knew like the back of his hand. "The key is to look for positions with high compensation but low actual time commitment," he reveals. "Some of my highest-paying roles required the least actual work—they were paying for my expertise and availability rather than constant output."

But the real genius of James's strategy wasn't in how he earned the money—it was in how he deployed it. Every paycheck was immediately divided according to a strict formula: 30% to index funds, 20% to real estate investments, 20% to his own tech startup, 20% to tax accounts, and 10% to liquid savings. Within three years, his investment portfolio had grown to over $2 million, and his startup had secured its first round of venture funding.

The pattern repeats across the upper tier of OE practitioners: the multiple jobs serve not as an end in themselves, but as rocket fuel for broader financial ambitions. Michelle, who maintained three product management positions simultaneously, used her combined income of $520,000 to launch a successful commercial real estate investment company. "OE is the only way this would have worked," she notes. "Managing multiple corporate roles teaches you exactly how to identify inefficiencies and opportunities in any market."

What separates these extreme practitioners from their peers isn't just their ability to manage multiple roles—it's their recognition that overemployment itself is a means to an end. They approach each position as a business would approach a new market opportunity, carefully calculating the return on time invested and the potential for knowledge arbitrage between roles.

Walter, who leveraged his experience managing five concurrent engineering positions into a consulting firm, now employs dozens of developers who were once colleagues at those jobs. "Each role taught me something different about how large organisations handle their technical challenges," he explains. "By the time I launched my own company, I had essentially completed a PhD in enterprise software development practices—and gotten paid millions to do it."

The financial strategies employed by these top performers often share common elements. Most maintain elaborate systems of separate bank accounts and LLCs to manage their income streams. They typically max out every available tax-advantaged investment vehicle—401(k)s, HSAs, backdoor Roth IRAs—across multiple employers. Many become experts in tax optimisation, working with specialised accountants to ensure their complex income situations don't result in unnecessary tax burdens.

"The goal isn't to hold these jobs forever," explains Rachel, who managed five concurrent roles in financial analysis before launching her own fintech startup. "The goal is to build enough momentum—financially and professionally—that you can choose your own path forward." Rachel's strategy involved using her multiple positions not just for income, but as a form of paid market research. Each role gave her insight into different aspects of the financial industry, eventually helping her identify the opportunity that would become her successful startup.

The investment patterns among extreme OE practitioners often follow a barbell strategy: highly conservative index fund investments on one end, balanced by aggressive bets on their own ventures on the other. This approach reflects their unique position—their multiple income streams provide enough security to take significant risks with a portion of their earnings.

The endgame varies among these high earners, but a common thread emerges: most view their period of extreme overemployment as a temporary means to achieve specific financial targets. Some, like Michael, set a strict number—"Five million in liquid investments was my exit number." Others use metrics like passive income: "I knew I was done when my investment income exceeded my highest-paying job's salary."

The timeline for these transformations can be surprisingly short. Among the most successful practitioners, two to three years of extreme overemployment often provides enough capital to fund their next phase, whether that's launching a business, building a real estate empire, or simply retiring to manage their investments. The key is having a clear exit strategy from the beginning.

"The biggest mistake people make is thinking of OE as a lifestyle," warns James. "At the extreme end, it's more like a sprint—incredibly intense, potentially very lucrative, but not sustainable indefinitely." His advice to newcomers is straightforward: "Know your number, have a plan for the money, and don't get seduced by the income alone."

The ripple effects of these success stories extend beyond individual practitioners. Many become informal mentors to others in the OE community, sharing insights about which industries and roles offer the best returns on time invested. Some, like Walter, eventually create businesses that explicitly hire and support other OE practitioners, understanding firsthand the value these professionals can provide.

The future of extreme overemployment remains uncertain. As more companies become aware of the practice, the opportunity window may narrow. Yet the lessons learned by these pioneers—about value creation, efficiency, and leveraging knowledge across contexts—have implications far beyond multiple job-holding.

For those considering following in these footsteps, the message from successful practitioners is clear: Extreme OE can be a powerful tool for building wealth, but it's the deployment of that wealth that ultimately determines success. The goal isn't to work multiple jobs forever—it's to work them strategically enough, and for long enough, to never have to work them again.

CHAPTER 12

MISTAKES AND COVER-UPS

Marissa was a seasoned recruiter with a keen eye for detail. She had been impressed with John throughout the interview process, but a discrepancy in his job history gave her pause. "Your job history shows two active positions," she said, her tone probing. John, quick to recover, claimed it was a clerical error. "Probably a mix-up in the records," he said smoothly.

Marissa wasn't convinced, but the company was in dire need of John's expertise. "I'll need you to clarify this in writing," she said. John sent the necessary email immediately. Despite her reservations, Marissa proceeded with the hire. A year later, John had proven to be an invaluable asset. Marissa's initial suspicion lingered in the back of her mind, but necessity had overshadowed her doubts. When she did finally learn the truth from a colleague who worked with John at his J2, she felt almost betrayed, yet somehow vindicated. She spent a lot of time asking herself if it really mattered, given his above-average work and consistency. In the end, his contributions outweighed the ethical dilemma.

To outsiders, the overemployed might appear to have superhuman discipline and an almost mechanical ability to avoid slip-ups. But in reality, managing two jobs is as much about handling mistakes as it is about avoiding them. Every day in the life of the overemployed carries the lurking possibility of a close call—a wrongly addressed email, a calendar clash, or a mix-up in meeting links. And while some risks can be managed with automation or careful planning, others demand split-second improvisation, an art of covering up on the fly, where recovery is key to survival.

Mike, a software developer who's mastered the quick reflexes required to dodge disaster in his dual roles. His first slip-up happened within weeks of starting his second job when he accidentally logged into the wrong Slack workspace to send a client update. The realisation was immediate, a heart-stopping moment as he saw the message flash onto the wrong team's feed. But Mike didn't panic. Instead, he quickly deleted the message, followed up with a light-hearted "Sorry, wrong chat!" and immediately shifted his status to "In a meeting" to divert any questions. It was a small blunder, but one that could've escalated without his quick thinking. This was a turning point, a reminder that overemployment isn't about avoiding all mistakes but learning to absorb, deflect, and move on without leaving traces.

The reality of overemployment is that mistakes are unavoidable, and so each professional develops their own arsenal of cover-up tactics. Mike, for example, has now created separate Slack profiles for each job, with different icons and display names for a quick visual reminder that keeps him from repeating that early mistake. Others, like

Kiera from Alaska, rely on segregated email clients and browsers to prevent crossovers, tagging each job with colour codes that highlight which email belongs to which employer. "Chrome for J1, Firefox for J2, Safari for J3. Nice and easy, you don't need to think about it any more than that. It's muscle memory." These aren't just precautionary steps—they're a survival mechanism, part of the mental scaffolding that allows the overemployed to perform their high-wire act without a net. Quick visual aids to remind them which audience they're talking to, reaching the cognitive overhead.

Yet, for every strategy and failsafe, there's always the unexpected. Priya is a data analyst who, after a long week, logged into the wrong company's meeting and was halfway through introducing herself before realising her mistake. She froze, then calmly explained that she was "just dropping by to check on the project status" before quickly excusing herself. Once out, she immediately sent a friendly email to her boss to clarify that she "just wanted to check they had an issue on the agenda I had asked about." The casual, confident nature of her cover-up, and channeling any suspicion about her odd behaviour toward the straw man issue worked, and the incident was forgotten by the next day. Priya's approach reflects a key truth among the overemployed: the more confident the response, the less likely people are to question it.

Overemployment often requires a level of discretion and secrecy that some find difficult to maintain. For Jake, a marketing specialist in Boston, it was his own hubris that nearly cost him everything. Jake had always been open about his side gigs. To him, they were a testament to his skills and versatility. When he landed a lucrative second job with a tech company in San Francisco, he couldn't resist bragging to a friend. This friend, however, had a loose tongue and a penchant for gossip.

It wasn't long before Jake received a call from his HR department at his primary job. An anonymous email had tipped them off about his dual employment. Panic set in. Jake scrambled to cover his tracks, deleting emails and messages, but the damage was done. HR demanded proof that the accusation was false. Jake played fast and loose with the facts, insisting that it was a baseless rumour started by an ex-colleague with a grudge.

Remarkably, Jake lied so convincingly that he managed to convince them, surprised that no one bothered to confirm anything he said. His primary job retained him, but the experience left him rattled. He realised that his loose talk had nearly cost him both jobs. Jake learned a harsh lesson about discretion and the thin line between confidence and arrogance.

The reality of dodging disaster also involves mental agility—a skill sharpened through necessity. Over time, the overemployed become adept at spotting early signs of trouble. They can tell when a project is getting too time-consuming, when a manager is growing suspicious, or when they've spread themselves too thin across overlapping responsibilities. And it's in these moments that their intuition becomes as vital as any technical skill. Rather than wait for issues to explode, they learn to pre-emptively defuse potential problems, managing expectations subtly but effectively. If they sense that one boss is becoming more demanding, they might "lean in" to that role slightly more for a week or two, creating breathing room in the other. This innate "drama radar" provides the ability to make minor shifts that put out small fires before they can take off.

Another critical skill in the overemployed toolkit is mastering "strategic transparency." Some overemployed workers find it beneficial to appear slightly overburdened, hinting at vague, "other projects" or "additional responsibilities" that provide an explanation for any occasional lapses. For example, Mike will occasionally mention "consulting work" outside his full-time job if he senses his manager is growing concerned with his availability. This creates a useful excuse for any sudden gaps in communication or last-minute requests for flexibility. By framing his life as one filled with "consulting responsibilities," he manages expectations, giving himself breathing room when his schedules collide or he needs to move something around. Not all full time workers have this flexibility however, with several cases involving employers who believe they have employees locked into exclusive contracted loyalty.

Tori's dual employment was a carefully guarded secret, known only to her closest confidants. But secrets have a way of surfacing. J1 needed her expertise for a contract, and so did J2. The overlap wasn't immediately obvious, but the small legal community in Texas made such coincidences inevitable. Tori's name appeared as the officiant on a contract for J1, and J2, seeing her name on a similar contract, demanded an update. Both companies realised they had been sharing the same employee.

The fallout was swift. Tori was summoned to HR meetings at both jobs. The threat of disbarment loomed large. Her career, meticulously built over years, now teetered on the edge of collapse. She posted her story anonymously online, hoping to warn others while grappling with her impending professional ruin. Tori's dilemma was a stark reminder of the risks inherent in overemployment. The irony of her situation was bitter—her skills and dedication, the very traits that made her valuable, had also been her undoing.

Mistakes aren't just logistical—they're emotional too. Each close call and minor error comes with a spike in adrenaline, a rush of fear that fades only with the resolution of the immediate problem. This cocktail of emotions is what keeps the overemployed so sharp—acutely aware of their every move. To thrive in this space, they learn not just to manage risk but to embrace it, to accept that while a life with multiple jobs is inherently unstable, it's a source of heightened focus and clarity. Many find this unpredictability exhilarating, because it's a constant test of their adaptability and wit. Like a chess game with management. Man vs The Machine. Over time, the mistakes and cover-ups become almost routine, a natural part of the landscape they negotiate daily.

Mistakes also aren't always failures for the average overemployment enjoyer. Just waypoints, reminders where to zig or zag a little earlier next time around. For every misstep, there's an opportunity to become just a little bit better at the game.

CHAPTER 13

THE ETHICAL LANDSCAPE

Tom sat at his physical J1 desk with a document from J2 open on his screen, confused.

It wasn't unusual for emails to cross wires occasionally in his long, tenured history of overemployment. Rising through the ranks of two related companies to manage a division in each, his dual employment had long been an open secret, and now even an asset—sitting on the boards of both, and acting as something of a liaison as they prepared to merge. This email was something different, however.

It was from Emma, one of his direct reports. But the attachment was clearly from her work at his J2. He wasn't even aware that she had been hired, and if he had been, he would have warned her to watch out for situations precisely like this.

Tom sighed, leaning back in his chair. Emma's phone call came within minutes, her voice a mix of panic and guilt. "I'm so sorry, Tom. That attachment was from my other job. I hope you don't mind that I'm moonlighting, but it's getting tough just to keep the lights on right now."

Tom could sense her anxiety through the phone. "I personally don't see a conflict," he said slowly, "but others in the company might. Just be more careful in the future. If you get caught again, I'll deny this conversation ever happened." Emma's relief was palpable, but Tom's warning was clear. He had no intention of covering for her should she slip up again. As he ended the call, Tom reflected on the irony. Emma was one of his best employees, yet her precarious balancing act threatened to undermine her professional standing. Tom knew he had been fair, but he also understood the unspoken tension that would now colour their interactions going forward.

The rise of overemployment has sparked more than just quiet conversations in remote corners of the internet; it's ignited a battle in boardrooms and HR departments across the globe. For employers, the idea of an employee secretly managing two or more jobs is not just a breach of trust—it's a violation of the unspoken social contract that has underpinned the modern workplace for decades. And as the overemployment trend grows, companies are pushing back, using legal frameworks, government systems, and corporate surveillance to regain control.

Laura was a project manager at a large financial services company, known for her organisational prowess and ability to deliver complex projects on time. Unbeknownst to her employer, she also held a second job as a consultant for a boutique firm. Laura managed to keep her dual roles a secret for over a year, deftly balancing her responsibilities and excelling in both positions.

The trouble began when Laura's primary employer implemented a new compliance policy, requiring all employees to disclose any outside employment. Laura, aware of the potential repercussions, chose not to disclose her consulting gig. However, an internal audit flagged her for further scrutiny, and her secret was eventually uncovered.

Laura found herself in a precarious legal situation. Her employment contract with the financial services company included a non-compete clause, which prohibited her from engaging in any employment with a competitor. Although the boutique firm operated in a different niche, the legal department at her primary job argued that her consulting work constituted a breach of contract.

Faced with potential legal action, Laura sought legal counsel to navigate the murky waters. Her lawyer argued that the non-compete clause was overly broad and unenforceable, given the different sectors in which the two companies operated. The case escalated to a legal battle, with both sides presenting compelling arguments.

In the end, the court ruled in Laura's favour, finding that the non-compete clause was indeed too broad and not applicable to her consulting work. However, the victory came at a significant cost. The legal fees and the stress of the proceedings took a toll on Laura, and she ultimately decided to leave both jobs to avoid further complications.

From the employer's perspective, overemployment is often framed as theft—not of physical goods or direct resources, but of attention, loyalty, and what they believe to be undivided commitment. As it becomes a more known and recognised phenomenon worldwide, employers are also strategising in dedicated groups around overemployment.

For decades, the employer-employee relationship has been built on an implicit unipolar understanding dictated by the employer: you work for us, and in exchange, we provide stability, resources, and opportunities for growth. But the rise of remote work has eroded the boundaries that once kept employees tethered to a single organisation. For the overemployed, loyalty is no longer a sacred bond—it's a calculated decision, contingent on how much value the employer provides, and how much leverage the worker can wield.

Employers, understandably, see things differently. To them, overemployment represents a fundamental betrayal of their trust. It's not just about the work employees are doing (or failing to do)—it's about what overemployment signals: that the job is just a means to an end, not a shared mission or mutual commitment. Even their most sacred of work, the full-time role, has been ingested into the "gig economy" race to bottom they themselves initiated. This mindset shift has left many employers scrambling to reassert control, often using aggressive tactics to uncover and punish overemployed workers.

Dan, a software engineer, was well-versed in the intricacies of technology and coding. He prided himself on his ability to solve complex problems and deliver innovative solutions. Dan's expertise made him a valuable asset to his employer, a leading tech company. However, his skills were also in high demand, leading him to take on a second job with a startup.

Dan was meticulous in his work, ensuring that he did not violate any confidentiality agreements or intellectual property rights. He believed that as long as he kept the two jobs separate, he was not breaching any legal obligations. However, the lines began to blur when both companies started working on similar projects involving cutting-edge artificial intelligence.

One evening, while reviewing code for the startup, Dan realised that a particular algorithm he had developed for his primary job could significantly benefit the project he was working on. Torn between his contractual obligations and the desire to excel in both roles, Dan decided to modify the algorithm slightly and implement it at the startup.

His decision came back to haunt him when his primary employer discovered the similarities in the code. An internal investigation revealed that Dan had used proprietary knowledge from his primary job in his work for the startup, leading to accusations of breach of confidentiality and intellectual property theft.

Dan faced severe legal repercussions. His primary employer terminated his contract and filed a lawsuit for damages, alleging that his actions had compromised their competitive edge. The startup, wary of the legal battle, also terminated his employment to distance themselves from the controversy.

The legal battle was long and gruelling, with Dan ultimately settling out of court. The financial and reputational damage was significant, and Dan's career took a severe hit. His story serves as a cautionary tale about the importance of understanding and adhering to confidentiality agreements and intellectual property laws in the context of overemployment.

As overemployment has grown more common, so too have the methods for detecting and combating it. Employers are leveraging a combination of government systems, private agencies, and advanced surveillance tools to identify dual-role workers.

One of the most effective tools in this arsenal is The Work Number, a third-party verification service that aggregates employment data from millions of workers. By cross-referencing payroll information, employers can uncover instances of overlapping jobs—a common hallmark of overemployment. Similarly, companies are increasingly relying on recurring background checks not just for pre-employment screening but for ongoing monitoring, ensuring that employees aren't moonlighting without disclosure.

Government systems also play a role, particularly in countries with robust tax reporting requirements. In the United States, discrepancies in W-2 forms or 1099 filings can raise red flags, prompting audits or inquiries that inadvertently reveal overemployment. Internationally, cross-border workers face even greater scrutiny, as conflicting tax filings across jurisdictions can trigger investigations. Many countries tax a second full time job at a much higher rate, requiring fully up-to-date disclosure of a citizen's work arrangements ,which may also, in some cases, be accessed by current employers and used to prove overemployment, triggering dismissal.

Perhaps the most contentious tool in the employer's arsenal is surveillance technology. From keystroke monitoring to video recording software, companies are investing heavily in tools that track employee productivity in real time. Ostensibly implemented to improve efficiency, these systems often double as covert means of identifying employees who may be dividing their attention between multiple roles.

Not all legal issues stem from the actions of the overemployed individuals themselves. Sometimes, the legal quagmire involves employer retaliation and the lengths to which companies will go to protect their interests.

In the case of a marketing executive named Mark who successfully managed two jobs for over two years, his primary employer—a multinational corporation—was none the wiser about his second role at a competing firm. Mark's dual employment came to light when a disgruntled colleague at the competing firm reported him to both companies.

The primary employer, feeling betrayed and concerned about potential conflicts of interest, decided to make an example of Mark. They terminated his contract and filed a lawsuit, accusing him of breach of fiduciary duty and theft of trade secrets. The competing firm, caught in the crossfire, also terminated his employment to avoid any legal entanglements.

Mark's legal battle was a high-stakes game of corporate vengeance. His primary employer sought to recoup financial damages and deter other employees from engaging in overemployment. The case attracted media attention, turning Mark into a cautionary example of the perils of overemployment.

In court, Mark's defence hinged on the argument that he had not disclosed any trade secrets or confidential information. His legal team argued that the primary employer's actions were retaliatory and designed to intimidate other employees. The court ruled in Mark's favour on some counts, but the financial and emotional toll was immense.

Mark's experience underscores the potential for employer retaliation in cases of overemployment. The legal ramifications can extend beyond mere contract violations, encompassing broader issues of corporate strategy and employee relations.

At its core, the legality of overemployment depends on the contracts that govern the employer-employee relationship. While few laws explicitly prohibit dual employment, many employment agreements contain clauses that restrict it, either through non-compete agreements, moonlighting policies, or exclusivity clauses.

Non-compete agreements, for instance, are designed to prevent employees from working for competitors during or after their tenure. In the United States, the enforceability of these agreements varies widely by state. California, for example, largely invalidates non-competes, while states like Texas and New York uphold them with few exceptions. Internationally, the landscape is equally fragmented— European countries often impose strict limits on non-competes, requiring employers to compensate employees for lost opportunities, whereas countries like India enforce them with fewer restrictions.

Moonlighting policies are more straightforward. Many companies explicitly prohibit secondary employment, even in unrelated industries, under the guise of preventing conflicts of interest. Violating these policies can lead to immediate dismissal, regardless of whether the secondary job interferes with primary responsibilities.

For the overemployed, navigating these legal frameworks requires both caution and interpretive creativity. Contract clauses must be carefully reviewed, and secondary roles chosen strategically to avoid direct conflicts with primary employers.

The legal and logistical challenges of overemployment are compounded by an equally complex ethical debate. For employers, the argument is clear: overemployment undermines team cohesion, diverts focus from organisational goals, and erodes the trust necessary for effective collaboration. Employees who work dual roles, they argue, are effectively freeloading, taking full salaries while delivering only partial effort.

Overemployed workers, however, see the issue differently. To them, the modern workplace has already broken the social contract, with companies prioritising profits over people and treating workers as disposable assets. Layoffs, stagnant wages, and exploitative practices have eroded the moral high ground employers once claimed, leaving workers to fend for themselves in an increasingly unstable economy. Overemployment, from this perspective, isn't a betrayal—it's survival.

The critique of overemployment as disloyalty or divided attention raises a stark question of fairness. Why is it acceptable—celebrated, even—for executives to sit on multiple corporate boards, serve as advisors to startups, or run side ventures while retaining their primary roles? These individuals are often heralded as visionaries, praised for their ability to juggle vast responsibilities. Their loyalty is rarely, if ever, questioned, even when they dedicate significant portions of their time to other organisations.

Take the example of board memberships. It is not uncommon for C-suite executives to hold seats on three, four, or even five boards, earning hefty compensation for their insights while ostensibly managing the complexities of their full-time executive roles. This division of focus, though undeniable, is framed as evidence of their capacity to manage complexity and exercise strategic judgment across domains. Yet, when an employee at a lower level takes on a second job, the narrative shifts to accusations of dishonesty, neglect, or even theft of attention.

This double standard highlights a hierarchy of presumed capability, where those at the top are trusted to handle multiple priorities, while workers further down are treated as though they cannot be trusted with complexity or competing interests. It's an implicit assumption of irresponsibility—a paternalistic view that suggests lower-level employees are less equipped to manage their time and commitments.

The reality is that many overemployed workers are just as capable of handling complexity as their executive counterparts. They juggle dual roles not out of greed but necessity, often delivering exceptional results in both positions. For these workers, overemployment isn't a betrayal of trust but a demonstration of adaptability, resourcefulness, and efficiency. They argue that the loyalty demanded by companies should be reciprocal. How can employers insist on undivided commitment from employees while offering little in return—no guarantees of job security, fair wages, or equitable treatment?

This imbalance feeds into a broader critique of corporate power dynamics. If organisations truly valued loyalty, they would foster it by creating environments where employees felt secure, respected, and adequately compensated. Instead, many workers see overemployment as a logical response to a system that prioritises profits over people, leaving them no choice but to prioritise their own interests.

For the overemployed, this isn't about undermining their employers—it's about reclaiming autonomy in a system that often treats them as interchangeable cogs. If executives are free to leverage their skills and time across multiple organisations, why shouldn't the rest of the workforce be afforded the same freedom? This question doesn't just challenge the ethics of overemployment; it challenges the ethics of the entire corporate hierarchy.

Which might be why this tension between corporate expectations and individual autonomy sits at the core of the overemployment debate. And as more workers embrace dual roles in the expanding gig economy, the ethical lines will only grow blurrier, forcing both sides to grapple with uncomfortable questions about loyalty, fairness, and the future of work.

As companies tighten their grip and workers push the boundaries of what's possible, overemployment will remain a contentious issue in the modern workplace. For employers, the challenge is clear: how to maintain control in a world where remote work has decentralised authority. For overemployed workers, the stakes are even higher. Juggling dual roles without crossing legal or ethical lines, hemmed in by more regulation, company policy, and ethical quandary than any other type of worker—requiring constant vigilance, adaptability, and a deep understanding of the systems at play.

The legal landscape of overemployment is as complex as it is volatile, shaped by conflicting interests, evolving technologies, and a rapidly changing economy. For those navigating this terrain, the path forward is about staying ahead of detection, abreast of legal and company statutes, and an ear to the ground in general, while participating in the redefinition of the very nature of work itself.

CHAPTER 14

CULTIVATING IDENTITY

We've explored how overemployment demands a high level of mental flexibility, and the capacity to shift seamlessly between identities in real time.

For the overemployed, this is an art form honed through practice, patience, and a willingness to embrace the cognitive strain that comes from embodying multiple personas within a single workday.

Each role they assume brings its own expectations, culture, and demands, requiring them to not only "wear different hats" but embody and project entirely distinct professional selves.

Jenna, a senior graphic designer who manages two roles in wildly different industries—one for a cutting-edge tech startup and the other for a well-established healthcare organisation—is a good example. The tech startup is fast-paced, agile, and thrives on innovation; Jenna's creative freedom there is encouraged, even celebrated. In contrast, her healthcare role is restrained, meticulous, and governed by compliance standards. Where one job allows her to experiment with bold colours and avant-garde layouts, the other expects her to follow stringent branding guidelines with almost surgical precision. And while Jenna revels in the chance to exercise different aspects of her design skills, this duality also requires intense focus—a constant recalibration between roles where the stakes are high and each misstep could trigger suspicion.

Jenna's mental flexibility is what makes this lifestyle possible. Her day begins with a simple ritual: a mental check-in where she reviews the key demands of each job, assesses her daily deadlines, and reminds herself of the subtle differences in tone, expectations, and interpersonal styles each role requires. She'll review her Slack conversations and skim through her emails to remind herself of ongoing projects in each role. This pre-emptive priming helps her slip into each identity seamlessly, preparing her for the day's meetings and creative tasks without hesitation. But it's a habit born from necessity, not ease. "By noon, I've had to remind myself who I am multiple times," Jenna laughs, "but that's just part of the game."

For those navigating multiple identities, compartmentalisation is essential. Over time, they become adept at building invisible walls between their roles, mentally fencing off each job to prevent information, style, and persona from bleeding across. But even this skill has its limits. There are moments when identities collide, a subtle but disorienting overlap that threatens to pull the entire act apart.

Alexis is a UX researcher who balances roles at two competing software companies. Each has its own distinct culture, lingo, and market positioning, and as he attends back-to-back meetings, the act of switching from one vocabulary set to another can be jarring. When one company refers to customers as "users" and the other prefers "clients," Alexis has to be vigilant, taking extra care not to slip in the wrong term. The smallest linguistic error could tip off an attentive colleague, so Alexis maintains a running mental list of each company's preferred terminology, a silent cheat sheet he's always updating.

This cognitive dexterity isn't something they can turn off after hours. Jenna recalls how her mindset shifts have seeped into her personal life, leading her to question her own authenticity. "Sometimes I'll go out with friends and feel this weird urge to be more casual and laid-back, only to realise I'm slipping into my tech job persona. I don't even know if I'm the same person I was before all this." It's a common sentiment among the overemployed—the sense that their multiple professional selves start to define them, overshadowing the individual beneath. They live in a constant state of adaptation, aware that each role brings with it its own mannerisms, attitudes, and expectations, and that keeping these elements compartmentalised is crucial to maintaining the illusion.

But for all its challenges, this identity-juggling act comes with its own rewards. Many overemployed individuals experience a kind of cognitive growth that's hard to find in a single job. The constant shifts between roles stretch their adaptability, forcing them to think on multiple levels, cultivate diverse perspectives, and master the subtle art of self-presentation. Each day becomes a mental workout, a series of rapid adjustments that sharpen their emotional intelligence, broaden their social dexterity, and strengthen their ability to perform under pressure. Jenna jokes that she's now capable of switching from "innovative disruptor" to "meticulous executor" in under a minute, a skill she never would have developed if she'd stayed in one role.

But the toll on mental health is real, too. Many overemployed workers experience a form of identity fatigue, a psychological exhaustion that stems from embodying so many personas. The boundaries between roles can start to blur, making it difficult to fully disconnect or "come home" to themselves at the end of the day. For some, the solution lies in strict routines—practices that help them recalibrate and separate each identity when the workday ends. Others, like Alexis, turn to hobbies that bring them back to a state of authenticity. He's taken up photography, finding solace in capturing scenes through his own eyes, unfiltered by the corporate personas he must inhabit during the day. "When I'm out with my camera, I don't have to think about who I'm supposed to be," he explains. "It's my reset button."

This identity compartmentalisation, while demanding, also provides an unexpected benefit: resilience. Over time, the overemployed learn to thrive under pressure, their minds growing sharper and more agile with each identity shift. They become adept at reading people, detecting nuances, and adapting their communication styles in ways that many traditional workers rarely need to consider. It's a mental agility that, while challenging, gives them a sense of control, a feeling that they're not just surviving but actively shaping their own professional destinies.

At the heart of this mental juggling act is a quiet satisfaction, a belief that for all the strain and complexity, they are proving something essential about the nature of work, identity, and self-determination. For those who can manage it, the rewards are more than just financial—they represent a victory over the limitations of conventional employment, a testament to the power of adaptability, and a rare kind of freedom that comes not from escaping the demands of work, but from mastering them on their own terms.

Cultivating an impeccable professional image across multiple roles is like walking a tightrope. It's a calculated, ongoing performance where perception becomes reality. It becomes quickly obvious that success hinges not only on productivity, but on curating a persona that inspires confidence, one that managers and colleagues trust implicitly. This persona is polished, reliable, and slightly elusive—a careful construction that allows them to manage multiple jobs without ever arousing suspicion. For the overemployed, image isn't just about impressing others; it's about creating a protective shell, a buffer that keeps probing questions and unwanted scrutiny at bay.

David is an account executive juggling two demanding sales roles. At J1, he's known as a results-driven powerhouse, and at J2, a calm and analytical strategist. His colleagues at each job have come to rely on his distinct approach, and each team sees him as indispensable. Yet, what they don't know is that David is managing not just two sets of clients but two entirely separate client databases, daily sales targets, and even two different sets of performance metrics. David's success isn't accidental—it's the result of a meticulously crafted professional image, one that's convincing enough to keep both companies satisfied, allowing him to maintain high visibility while simultaneously guarding his true circumstances.

The overemployed learn early that perception is, in many ways, more important than reality. If you appear reliable and dedicated, people tend to assume that you are. For David, this means maintaining a steady flow of communications, hitting key performance metrics, and delivering on promises with precision. He understands that visibility is not about constant presence but about being visible when it counts. A well-timed message here, a supportive comment in a meeting there, and he's created the impression of someone who's constantly engaged, even when he's shifting focus between roles. This "strategic visibility" isn't just about performing for others; it's a safety net that allows him to shift seamlessly between his identities without drawing attention to gaps.

Yet curating a flawless image isn't just about when and how he shows up; it's also about knowing when to step back. David recognises that overexposure can be as dangerous as invisibility. He'll occasionally block out "deep work" time, a well-understood concept in modern work culture, using it as a cover for hours when he needs to focus on the other job. This "deep work" time allows him to duck out of impromptu meetings and sidestep spontaneous conversations without raising suspicion. Ironically, David's dedication to guarding his image requires a level of discretion that borders on artistry.

To many overemployed workers, LinkedIn is both a resource and a hazard. It's one of the most public faces they have, a space where any inconsistency can unravel their carefully crafted image. LinkedIn updates, profile tweaks, even new skills or recommendations—each move must be carefully measured to ensure it aligns with the identity they've curated. Some, like Emma, a project manager, go so far as to create separate, tailored LinkedIn profiles, each with vague titles that hint at consultancy rather than specific full-time roles. Her profiles are carefully maintained but never updated in tandem, avoiding any overlap that could catch the attention of mutual connections.

But curating an image goes beyond LinkedIn or Slack statuses. It extends to email tone, message cadence, and meeting behaviours. For instance, Emma has honed the art of "email echoing," a technique where she mirrors her managers' communication styles. If one manager prefers formal, structured emails, her replies are crisp and structured. If the other manager tends toward casual updates peppered with emojis, she matches that tone as well. This subtle mirroring isn't just polite; it's a method of aligning herself seamlessly within each company culture, establishing herself as someone who "gets it"—and by extension, someone who doesn't require close supervision.

These curated images protect the overemployed from suspicion and even from the burden of unmanageable expectations. They've become adept at creating personas that are highly competent but not indispensable, skilled but never so specialised that they'd attract attention from senior leadership. The goal is always to be valuable enough to keep around but never so irreplaceable that anyone looks too closely at their workload.

For Tommo, a software engineer with dual roles in development, this image curation extends to the work itself. He's learned that some projects demand visibility, while others benefit from being quietly completed in the background. By selectively highlighting his involvement in projects that are timely and high-impact, he ensures his managers are aware of his value. But for lower-stakes projects or routine updates, he keeps his participation more subdued, allowing him to fly under the radar while freeing up time for the other job. This approach allows him to present a consistent record of performance without the risk of overextending himself in either role.

However, maintaining multiple professional images isn't without its pressures. For the overemployed, each carefully crafted persona becomes a mental costume, one they slip into each morning with the same precision as clocking in. It requires them to embody an idealised version of themselves —a hybrid between high performance and strategic invisibility. Some, like Emma, experience moments where this duality feels overwhelming, a psychological strain that forces them to question which version of themselves is real. It's a balancing act where the weight of each identity can feel crushing, yet the rewards keep them steady on the tightrope.

In a sense, the overemployed are pioneers, navigating uncharted territory where personal branding becomes a survival mechanism. They understand that their work is seen through the lens of perception, and by carefully controlling that perception, they gain a measure of power over their professional lives that traditional workers rarely experience. For many, this life of constant curation becomes almost second nature, a part of their daily existence that, while exhausting, also offers a peculiar sense of satisfaction. They're playing a game of perception, one where they write the rules, set the pace, and ultimately, control the outcome.

In the end, curating this perfect professional image is not just about fooling others—it's about reclaiming control over one's career, about realising that the structures of work are more malleable than they once believed. The overemployed have learned that image, far from being a shallow construct, is a powerful tool for shaping reality, a reminder that in today's digital world, appearances are more than just surface-level—they're a gateway to opportunity. And for those willing to take the risk, they're a path to a new kind of freedom.

CHAPTER 15

HIGH-STAKES CONVERSATIONS

For the overemployed, conversations with managers and colleagues become a strategic exercise, a carefully measured blend of confidence, deflection, and controlled openness. These aren't ordinary exchanges—they're high-stakes interactions where saying too much or too little could lead to suspicion. Every word counts, every pause calculated. And over time, the overemployed develop an instinct for this dialogue, honing their ability to navigate questions, dodge unwelcome scrutiny, and keep both employers satisfied without tipping their hand.

Zoe is a product manager in two high-stakes roles, one with a digital media company and another with a fintech startup. In both companies, her work involves frequent meetings, strategic planning sessions, and weekly one-on-ones with senior leadership. To her managers, Zoe is the epitome of composure, someone who "always seems to have everything under control." Little do they know that she's balancing two roles, seamlessly weaving responses to fit each company's distinct culture and expectations. Zoe's approach to conversations is like playing a well-practiced hand of cards; she knows precisely when to reveal details, when to withhold, and when to nod thoughtfully to convey a level of engagement that keeps questions at bay.

In high-stakes conversations, the overemployed know that authenticity is essential, but selective authenticity is paramount. Rather than over-explaining absences or unusual scheduling needs, they rely on broad, generally accepted excuses that hold up without much elaboration. Zoe often uses vague but universally understood reasons like "family responsibilities" or "doctor's appointments" to justify rescheduling meetings or taking time off, phrases that tend to end conversations rather than invite further inquiry. By keeping explanations short and to the point, she leaves little room for probing questions, presenting an image of professionalism that managers are more inclined to respect than question.

But high-stakes conversations aren't just about managing suspicion; they're also about steering expectations. Karl is an account executive juggling two sales roles. He's mastered the art of "proactive positioning," a technique that involves setting subtle boundaries through conversational cues. For instance, he'll frequently mention that he's "focusing on high-priority accounts" in conversations with his managers, subtly conveying that his attention may be divided without giving any concrete reason for it. This phrase not only positions him as a high-value employee but also implicitly sets a limit on his availability, allowing him to keep some flexibility without explicitly stating it. It's a balancing act of suggestion and implication, one that enables him to maintain control over his time without inviting unnecessary scrutiny.

Timing, too, is a critical component of the overemployed conversational skill set. They learn when to bring up topics that might seem unusual, carefully choosing moments that are least likely to trigger suspicion. Jenna, the graphic designer, has an instinct for bringing up "personal commitments" in meetings right before major project deadlines, knowing that colleagues are more focused on the deliverables than her personal schedule. She uses this timing to her advantage, planting just enough context to justify potential absences without causing alarm. By strategically aligning her explanations with the ebb and flow of her work's natural rhythm, she's able to avoid deeper inquiries and remain in good standing with both teams.

This ability to steer conversations extends to written communication as well. Overemployed workers like Zoe and Karl often tailor their email styles based on the recipient, using different tones and levels of detail depending on whether they're writing to a direct supervisor, a peer, or a team member in another department. Zoe has perfected the art of "layered responses," where she crafts emails that can be skimmed quickly by managers for key points, yet contain enough detail to satisfy any deeper reading. This not only protects her from questions but also allows her to set her own pace for follow-up tasks, giving her breathing room in a tight schedule. It's a calculated dance of clarity and brevity that requires a high degree of skill, but for Zoe, it's second nature.

There's also an element of intuition involved, a finely tuned sense of when a question might be harmless curiosity or something more probing. Overemployed professionals become masters of reading between the lines, sensing when someone is genuinely interested in their well-being or when they might be poking around. This intuition often leads to pre-emptive countermeasures—small conversational detours that subtly change the subject or redirect attention. If Karl senses his manager is digging a little too deeply into his schedule, he'll pivot to a discussion of recent sales wins or a new strategy he's implemented, effectively shifting the focus to his performance. These detours are strategic and reflexive, executed with a practiced ease that makes them virtually undetectable.

Yet, for all their finesse, these high-stakes conversations come with a cost. Constantly filtering information, maintaining mental walls between roles, and staying vigilant against missteps is exhausting. The overemployed are well aware of the tightrope they walk, and for some, the weight of these constant mental calculations becomes a burden. Ingrid, for example, often finds herself mentally replaying conversations after the fact, scrutinising every word to ensure she didn't slip up. It's a level of attention that borders on hyper-vigilance, a heightened awareness that can leave even the most skilled feeling drained.

But for those who can handle the pressure, this conversational agility offers a strange satisfaction, a feeling of control that extends beyond work and into their lives. Many find themselves applying these skills outside the office, developing a nuanced communication style that translates to personal relationships, social gatherings, even casual interactions with strangers. They become, in a sense, adept at navigating the unwritten rules of conversation, a skill that proves as valuable as any technical ability.

Ultimately, the art of high-stakes conversation isn't just about keeping their jobs hidden—it's about crafting a reality in which they're able to flourish on their own terms. Each successful conversation becomes a victory, each smooth deflection a testament to their adaptability. And for those walking this path, the payoff goes beyond the financial; it's about proving, day by day, that they have mastered a level of control, resilience, and ingenuity that conventional careers rarely require. This is the ultimate satisfaction of the overemployed life—not just the ability to work multiple jobs but the capacity to manage them with a grace and subtlety that leaves even the keenest observer none the wiser.

CHAPTER 16

SLOW BURN IMPOSTER SYNDROME

For all the careful planning, calculated risks, and confident conversations, overemployment often comes with an unavoidable psychological weight: imposter syndrome. It's a quiet but pervasive feeling, creeping in during the brief moments between meetings, or late at night, as the overemployed reflect on a day spent navigating double lives. While imposter syndrome is a common experience in any career, for the overemployed, it becomes amplified, compounded by the knowledge that they are, in essence, concealing a part of themselves from every single colleague.

Consider Samira, a systems analyst juggling two full-time roles, one in a fast-paced cybersecurity firm and another in a consultancy focusing on cloud infrastructure. By all outward appearances, she's thriving. She meets deadlines, contributes insightful solutions, and receives regular praise from both teams. Yet, each accolade lands with a hollow ring, echoing against her internal sense of misalignment. No matter how high she climbs in each role, a part of her feels fraudulent, as if at any moment someone will see through her carefully constructed personas and expose the ruse. It's a gnawing doubt that even her most impressive accomplishments can't fully erase.

For Samira, and others like her, imposter syndrome doesn't just stem from the high expectations of each role—it's a byproduct of constantly shifting identities, never being able to fully belong to either team. In meetings, she catches herself withholding suggestions, cautious not to bring too much of her own personality or ideas forward, fearing that doing so might make her dual commitments too obvious. This self-imposed restraint, while necessary, can create a sense of isolation, as if she's perpetually on the outside looking in, never quite able to let down her guard. Even when she's fully engaged in a task, there's always a piece of her mind occupied with managing the next move, guarding against the tiniest slip.

This constant vigilance erodes her confidence, creating an internal feedback loop where doubt feeds into performance, and performance feeds back into doubt. After a day of meetings and multitasking, Samira often finds herself questioning if she's actually contributing anything meaningful to either job or if she's just skating by, doing just enough to appear valuable. It's a draining mental cycle, one that requires her to build herself back up daily, reminding herself that, despite her hidden double life, she is indeed capable, competent, and deserving of the roles she holds.

Yet, despite this internal dialogue, Samira finds solace in the structure she's built around her. She realises that her double role isn't simply a deception—it's a testament to her skills and discipline. Over time, she learns to reframe her imposter syndrome, viewing it less as a sign of inadequacy and more as a side effect of her ambitious path. She begins to see that her ability to juggle two demanding roles, each requiring unique skills, is proof of her competence. This shift in perspective doesn't eliminate her self-doubt, but it tempers it, reminding her that managing two jobs is not just a stroke of luck—it's a skill she's earned through hard work and resilience.

For other overemployed individuals, imposter syndrome manifests in subtler ways, eroding their sense of self-worth and making even routine tasks feel monumental. Consider Luke, a data scientist who balances two high-level roles in artificial intelligence. His work requires intense focus, creativity, and an ability to foresee potential issues before they arise. But even with a string of successful projects, he struggles to shake the feeling that he's only pretending to know what he's doing. Every accomplishment feels diminished by the fact that, in his mind, he's splitting his attention between two worlds, unable to commit fully to either. Each project he completes, each problem he solves, brings not just satisfaction but a twinge of anxiety—a sense that maybe he's cutting corners, that he isn't truly as competent as his colleagues believe.

The overemployed often find themselves creating mental lists of their perceived failings, cataloguing every tiny misstep as evidence that they're undeserving of their roles. This self-imposed scrutiny can be paralysing, leading some to doubt their own skills, even in areas where they have a proven track record. Luke catches himself holding back in meetings, downplaying his own ideas, convinced that speaking up might expose some unseen flaw or deficiency. And yet, the reality is that his dual roles are functioning smoothly, a fact he tries to remind himself of whenever the doubt creeps in.

For those grappling with imposter syndrome, the very act of balancing multiple jobs becomes a double-edged sword. On one hand, they are constantly proving their competence through careful management and strategic thinking; on the other, each success can feel tainted, as if it's only a matter of time before someone sees through the act. Some, like Samira and Luke, have learned to find support in their anonymous overemployment communities, connecting with others who share their experiences and offer reassurance. It's in these spaces that they find validation, reminders that imposter syndrome isn't unique to them but a common experience shared by anyone taking on an ambitious, unconventional path.

The emotional toll of imposter syndrome is real, but for many, it becomes a source of motivation, a reminder of why they're doing this in the first place. Over time, some develop ways to manage the doubt, embracing it as part of the journey rather than a sign of failure. They learn to take stock of their achievements, recognising that their ability to navigate the complexity of dual roles isn't just a survival mechanism—it's a skill, a testament to their adaptability. With each day, they become more resilient, more aware of their strengths, and ultimately more convinced of their own value.

For those who manage to push through, imposter syndrome doesn't vanish, but it transforms, becoming a quiet background hum rather than an overwhelming presence. And in this way, the overemployed learn to walk the line between self-doubt and self-assurance, finding balance not by eliminating their insecurities but by acknowledging them, reframing them, and using them as fuel for the challenging, ambitious path they've chosen to walk. The daily victories, the resilience gained, and the quiet satisfaction of mastering this dual life become their most potent antidote to imposter syndrome—a steady, incremental reminder that, despite the doubts, they belong here just as much as anyone else.

CHAPTER 17

RELATIONSHIPS IN THE SHADOWS

For many overemployed professionals, the demands of juggling multiple roles don't just weigh on their daily schedules or mental energy; they bleed into their personal relationships, subtly shifting the dynamics with friends, partners, and family members. The overemployed life requires not only time management but also a quiet solitude—a level of secrecy and compartmentalisation that can be isolating, even from the people they care about most. As they navigate this lifestyle, overemployed individuals often find themselves shouldering a unique kind of emotional burden, one that goes unseen by those closest to them and remains hidden, tucked beneath their professional personas.

Anna, a senior marketing manager who handles a dual role in two major corporations, knows this burden all too well. To her boyfriend, she's a dedicated professional who sometimes works long hours, but she's never revealed the full extent of her overemployment. While he knows she's ambitious and focused on her career, Anna has kept her second job hidden, not because she doesn't trust him but because she fears he wouldn't understand the complexities of her choice. It's a decision born from both practicality and self-protection, a way to keep her double life stable without introducing outside concerns. Yet, as time passes, Anna feels the quiet strain of maintaining this boundary, a wall that keeps her significant other at a slight distance, leaving parts of herself she cannot share.

For many in her situation, the choice to withhold such a major aspect of their lives isn't taken lightly. Relationships thrive on transparency, on a sense of shared experience, and the overemployed are well aware of the potential erosion of trust that secrecy can bring. Yet the stakes are high, and full disclosure can feel like a risk too great to take. Anna manages this divide with half-truths and vague mentions of "side work" or "extra projects," carefully crafted explanations that preserve her autonomy while offering just enough detail to keep questions at bay. But there are times when the secrecy weighs heavily, creating moments of loneliness that can feel all-consuming. At family gatherings or social events, she often catches herself filtering her stories, avoiding any mention of the other half of her work life, constantly aware of the mental partition she's built to protect her dual careers.

But it's not just partners and family members who are affected by this secrecy; friendships can become strained, too. Over time, the overemployed find themselves retreating from social gatherings, avoiding happy hours, dinners, and catch-ups that could disrupt their carefully maintained schedules. Ben, a UX lead balancing two remote jobs, has found that his social circle has gradually narrowed as he prioritises time for work over time with friends. He loves his friends dearly, but with back-to-back deadlines and constant demands on his attention, he's often too mentally drained to engage in casual socialising. Where he used to be the first to plan group outings, Ben now finds himself routinely turning down invitations, vaguely citing work obligations that his friends have come to view as a part of his "new normal."

This gradual distancing can create an unintended sense of alienation, as the overemployed drift further from social circles they once cherished. For Ben, this has led to an inner conflict, a quiet but persistent worry that he's sacrificing important connections in pursuit of financial goals. He's aware that friendships, unlike jobs, are irreplaceable, yet he often feels caught between the demands of work and the desire to maintain a healthy social life. And while his friends are understanding, he senses a subtle shift in the dynamics —a growing perception that he's chosen work over relationships, a notion that, while partially true, feels incomplete and misunderstood.

For those with children, the emotional toll is perhaps even more pronounced. Parenting while overemployed requires a delicate balancing act, one where professional and personal boundaries blur, and time becomes a precious, hard-fought commodity. Sarah, a project manager and mother of two, is no stranger to this struggle. She manages her dual roles during school hours and late into the night, carving out time for both her kids and her work responsibilities. To her children, she's present, attentive, and engaged—but Sarah often feels the strain of hiding her double life from them, aware that even a slight misstep could create unintended confusion. She's also painfully aware that every extra hour spent on work is an hour less spent with her family, a trade-off that, while financially rewarding, leaves her questioning the long-term impact on her children's lives.

In navigating this hidden lifestyle, the overemployed become masters of compartmentalisation, creating mental boxes where each part of their life fits neatly away from the others. Yet, this constant separation takes an emotional toll, one that, over time, can feel draining and unsustainable. For many, there's a quiet longing to share the burden with someone, to confide in a friend or loved one without fear of judgement or exposure. But the fear of misunderstanding or disapproval often keeps them silent, leaving them isolated in their dual roles, shouldering a secret they can't fully explain.

However, there are moments of connection that emerge in unexpected places. Some overemployed individuals find solace in online forums or anonymous chat groups where they can share their experiences freely, without the risk of judgement. In these communities, they find kindred spirits, people who understand the nuances of balancing relationships, secrecy, and the demands of multiple jobs. Anna, for instance, regularly checks into an online forum for overemployed professionals, where she finds a level of understanding and camaraderie that she can't find elsewhere. It's here that she shares the struggles of maintaining her double life, the guilt that comes with it, and the small victories that keep her motivated. For many, these virtual communities become a lifeline, a space where they can finally let down their guard and reveal the full scope of their experience.

Yet, even with this support, the emotional toll of overemployment remains a constant presence, a reminder of the compromises and sacrifices that come with this path. The overemployed learn to carry this weight with a quiet resilience, finding ways to navigate relationships in the shadows, balancing their personal connections with the secrecy required to protect their dual lives. It's a delicate dance, one that demands both discipline and introspection, as they strive to honour their ambitions without losing the connections that matter most.

Ultimately, the emotional toll of overemployment is a unique kind of loneliness, a feeling of being perpetually "other" in both personal and professional realms. For those who embrace this life, the challenge becomes not just about maintaining their careers but about finding a way to hold onto themselves and their relationships in the process. It's a path filled with complexities, a choice that requires constant reflection and a deep understanding of one's own values. And for those who walk this path, the journey is as much about resilience as it is about success, a testament to the strength required to navigate the hidden layers of a life lived in double.

CHAPTER 18

THE ART OF BOUNDARIES

For the overemployed, boundaries are no longer a luxury but a lifeline—a structured necessity that keeps their carefully balanced world intact. In a traditional work environment, boundaries are often fluid, shifting between personal time and professional obligations as required. But for the overemployed, with multiple roles vying for time and focus, boundaries are about preserving the very core of self in a landscape of conflicting demands and pressures. These aren't just professional boundaries; they're existential ones, a constant, almost meditative practice of staying anchored amidst the demands of a dual life.

The reality is that, without solid boundaries, the overemployed would quickly burn out, overwhelmed by the endless stream of notifications, the conflicting schedules, and the weight of holding two identities at once. But boundaries aren't a simple matter of saying "no" or setting limits on hours. They're an intricate dance, an act of strategic prioritisation that involves mental and emotional discipline. For those who make it work, it's an art form that balances ambition with self-care, control with surrender, and the ability to engage fully in both roles without losing themselves to either.

Nadia, a marketing strategist has perfected the art of compartmentalising her dual roles. At 9 a.m., she is entirely present in her role at a digital media agency, where she leads campaign brainstorming sessions and collaborates on strategies to improve engagement. By noon, she switches into her second role at a non-profit, slipping seamlessly into meetings about outreach and donor engagement, immersing herself in a completely different mission and tone. But Nadia's ability to manage these transitions goes far beyond calendar blocks; she has trained herself to build mental "doors" that separate her roles, creating distinct spaces in her mind for each job.

Nadia's routine isn't just about focus; it's a form of self-protection. She knows that without these mental doors, the responsibilities and stress of each job could easily bleed together, resulting in a chaotic overlap that would threaten her productivity and her sanity. To maintain this separation, she's developed rituals that help her transition from one role to another—a specific type of music she plays to signal the start of her second job, a different notebook for each role, and even a quick walk around her block to reset her mindset. These small acts, seemingly mundane, become profound symbols of her autonomy, a reminder that she controls the flow of her day, not the demands of her roles.

This art of boundaries extends beyond work hours and into Nadia's personal life. Like many overemployed professionals, she has found that setting clear boundaries with herself is just as important as those with her employers. She refuses to check her work emails outside of designated hours, a hard line she maintains regardless of the urgency of the messages. On weekends, she disengages entirely from both roles, devoting her time to personal pursuits that have nothing to do with her professional identities. Friends and family know that Nadia's weekends are sacred, that she's unreachable not because she's unavailable but because she's chosen, intentionally, to protect that time for herself.

Yet, for all her discipline, Nadia still feels the pull of her roles, the whisper of responsibility that lingers even in her off-hours. She describes it as a "phantom presence," a mental echo of her dual roles that's hard to completely silence. And it's this challenge that lies at the heart of overemployment—the subtle, ongoing struggle to remain grounded amidst the constant call to perform, the perpetual tension between productivity and peace. But Nadia, like many in the overemployed community, has found that boundaries aren't about total separation but about selective permeability, knowing when to allow work into her personal space and when to firmly shut it out.

This concept of selective permeability is critical for sustaining the overemployed lifestyle. It's the understanding that boundaries aren't static walls but fluid thresholds, adjusted and recalibrated based on the demands of each day. It requires a profound level of self-awareness, a willingness to assess one's own mental state, energy levels, and emotional bandwidth daily. For the overemployed, this self-awareness becomes a tool as vital as any technical skill or time management technique, enabling them to maintain a sense of self that goes beyond their professional identities.

Yet, creating and maintaining these boundaries isn't always straightforward. Trevor, a data scientist managing two remote roles, has struggled with guilt around his boundaries, particularly when it comes to his employers' expectations. Both jobs assume his full commitment, and although he's careful to meet all deadlines and deliver quality work, he often feels a lingering pressure to "do more," a sense of responsibility that conflicts with his need to protect his time. This guilt can create moments of self-doubt, a fear that he's failing to give either role his all. But Trevor has come to realise that boundaries, while sometimes uncomfortable, are essential to achieving the balance he needs. He reminds himself that his commitment is measured by his results, not by constant availability, and that protecting his boundaries ultimately allows him to perform better in both roles.

Boundaries, for the overemployed, are a form of self-respect, a recognition that they are more than just their work identities. By setting limits, they honour the parts of themselves that exist beyond productivity, beyond career achievements, beyond the expectations of employers. This practice of self-preservation becomes a quiet rebellion against a work culture that often equates worth with output, a reminder that they define their own value, independent of the roles they play.

In the end, the art of boundaries is about finding freedom within the structure of overemployment. It's the ability to step back, to rest, to remember that their lives are more than a series of tasks and deadlines. For the overemployed, boundaries are not about restriction; they're about liberation, a way to create a life that is rich and varied, one where work is balanced with rest, ambition with contentment, and where the self remains intact, unclaimed by the demands of any single role.

This is the paradox of overemployment: the choice to take on more doesn't diminish their need for space but deepens it, creating an even greater need to guard their time, their peace, and their sense of self. And in mastering this art, they find a strength and resilience that goes far beyond professional success—a testament to the power of boundaries not just as a skill, but as a way of life.

CHAPTER 19

THRIVING IN CONTROLLED CHAOS

The overemployed life is one of constant, controlled chaos. Balancing multiple roles doesn't just require time management or technical skills; it demands a profound resilience, a mental fortitude to navigate the relentless pace, the tight deadlines, and the unspoken stress that shadows every task. For those who succeed, resilience becomes more than just a buzzword—it's a finely tuned internal mechanism, a system they build to maintain stability while the demands of dual lives pull them in different directions. And as they learn to adapt, the overemployed often find themselves thriving under pressure, developing a kind of invincibility that extends beyond work and into every part of their lives.

In many ways, resilience for the overemployed is like a muscle, strengthened over time by exposure to daily stressors. Lauren is a business analyst who spends her days moving between two complex roles in financial consulting and software development. Each position demands intense focus, precision, and a quick adaptability that leaves little room for error. Early on, Lauren struggled with the sheer volume of work, her days blurring into a series of back-to-back meetings and high-stakes tasks. But as the weeks passed, she began to notice subtle shifts in her ability to manage stress. She no longer panicked when meeting requests overlapped, and deadlines that once felt insurmountable became manageable challenges. What had initially felt like chaos started to feel like a system, one that she was learning to control, layer by layer.

For Lauren, this resilience didn't come from sheer determination alone; it was a matter of creating a mental framework that allowed her to filter, process, and compartmentalise stress. She developed a series of small routines to bring order to her day—a quick five-minute meditation between meetings, a walk around her block at lunch, and a ritual of reviewing her achievements each evening. These practices became touchpoints, stabilisers that grounded her amidst the chaos. Over time, they transformed into resilience anchors, a set of habits that gave her the strength to face each day with renewed focus and confidence.

But resilience for the overemployed isn't just about self-soothing or stress management; it's about endurance, a capacity to sustain high performance across multiple domains without succumbing to exhaustion. Alex, a project manager with dual roles in marketing and product development, knows this well. His day begins at 7 a.m., checking project timelines and client deliverables for one job, before shifting to strategic planning and content creation for another. By evening, he's mentally drained, his mind racing with task lists, status updates, and future deadlines. Yet, instead of collapsing under the pressure, Alex has learned to channel his fatigue into what he calls "focused recovery."

For Alex, focused recovery is a form of active rest, a way of decompressing that keeps him mentally engaged without draining his energy reserves. It might mean listening to a podcast on his evening run, cooking a simple but rewarding meal, or watching a documentary that has nothing to do with work. These activities allow him to unwind without completely disconnecting, keeping his mind flexible, yet relaxed. In this way, Alex maintains a balance between work and rest, a subtle rhythm that helps him recharge without losing momentum. For the overemployed, resilience is not about ignoring fatigue but learning to recover on the go, finding pockets of restoration in the midst of continuous pressure.

This adaptability, this ability to thrive in controlled chaos, is perhaps one of the most unique qualities of the overemployed. They become experts at parsing through demands, identifying what truly matters, and letting go of non-essential tasks. Over time, their resilience becomes almost instinctual, a natural response to pressure that allows them to face challenges head-on. Lauren, for instance, no longer views her dual roles as a burden but as a catalyst for growth. She sees each deadline as an opportunity to refine her skills, each meeting as a chance to test her adaptability. Her resilience has evolved beyond survival; it's become a source of empowerment, a reminder that she's capable of far more than she once believed.

Yet, for all its strength, resilience in the overemployed isn't without its challenges. Many find themselves pushing to the edge of their limits, navigating a fine line between resilience and burnout. This balancing act requires constant self-assessment, an awareness of their own thresholds, and the ability to step back when the demands become too great. Those who sustain this lifestyle understand that resilience isn't about invincibility; it's about knowing when to push forward and when to rest, recognising that endurance is a long game, not a sprint.

For Lauren and Alex, this resilience has led to profound insights about their own capabilities. They've learned that resilience is less about enduring hardship and more about actively shaping their environment, creating systems and habits that allow them to thrive. They've become adept at boundary-setting, knowing that protecting their mental energy is just as important as completing tasks. And in doing so, they've gained a sense of control that extends beyond their professional lives, a feeling of self-mastery that touches every aspect of their existence.

Resilience, for the overemployed, becomes a philosophy, a way of approaching life with both ambition and restraint, a recognition that strength lies not in never faltering but in learning to rise again, and again, and again. It's a quiet form of courage, one that doesn't demand recognition but exists as a constant, a steady heartbeat that pulses beneath their dual lives. And as they grow stronger, more capable, the overemployed find that resilience becomes not just a skill but a way of being, a testament to the power of the human spirit to adapt, endure, and ultimately, to thrive.

CHAPTER 20

COMPOUND SKILL AMPLIFICATION

The overemployed lifestyle isn't merely about financial gain or the thrill of a double life. Beneath the carefully orchestrated schedules and meticulously crafted personas lies something deeper—a pursuit of mastery, a drive to sharpen their skills, broaden their knowledge, and push the boundaries of what they're capable of achieving. Overemployment becomes not just a survival strategy but a proving ground, a space where they test, refine, and amplify their abilities at a rate that would be unthinkable in a single job. This relentless pace, while demanding, offers a rare opportunity for rapid skill development, one that transforms the overemployed from ordinary professionals into multi-dimensional experts.

Consider Maya, a software engineer who manages two full-time coding roles: one for a SaaS startup focused on AI integration, and another at an established e-commerce platform. In her day-to-day work, Maya oscillates between languages, architectures, and development styles, learning to pivot between vastly different projects with each job. At the SaaS startup, her work is experimental, fast-paced, and encourages risk-taking, while her e-commerce role requires precision, stability, and a methodical approach to updates. Through this dual exposure, Maya's coding abilities have advanced at an extraordinary rate, her mind constantly stretched to adapt, analyse, and implement solutions across multiple technical frameworks. What would take years to learn in a traditional role, she's mastered in months, driven by the need to juggle the complexities of two demanding tech environments.

For Maya, this accelerated skill acquisition is one of the most rewarding aspects of overemployment. Each job acts as a learning lab, a testing ground where she applies lessons from one role to improve her performance in the other. She's become adept at finding shortcuts, discovering efficiencies, and identifying universal principles that make her a stronger coder in both roles. It's a process of synthesis, a continual blending of experiences that enhances her overall technical fluency and creative problem-solving. This relentless pace of learning and adaptation has led Maya to a profound realisation: her dual roles are not just jobs—they're master classes, and she is both student and instructor, shaping her skill set in ways that a single role could never provide.

Yet, this path to mastery isn't reserved for technical fields alone. Lucas, a financial analyst managing roles at a major investment bank and a fintech startup, has experienced similar growth in his expertise. His work involves balancing the traditional, risk-averse approach of the bank with the innovation-driven, data-intensive methods of fintech. On any given day, he might be building conservative financial models in the morning and delving into cryptocurrency analysis by the afternoon. Each environment presents a unique set of challenges, and Lucas has learned to toggle between cautious pragmatism and bold innovation, cultivating a dual perspective that has become his greatest asset. Through this process, he's not only refined his analytical abilities but has developed a nuanced understanding of the financial sector that transcends conventional industry silos.

For overemployed individuals like Maya and Lucas, the dual-job experience becomes an advanced curriculum, a highly concentrated form of learning that fast-tracks their careers in ways they never anticipated. But the benefits go beyond technical prowess; overemployment hones what might be called "meta-skills," those high-level abilities that underpin success in any field. Skills like time management, adaptability, strategic thinking, and emotional intelligence become finely tuned under the pressure of juggling multiple roles. Over time, the overemployed find themselves not only mastering their specific job functions but developing a mental agility that allows them to approach problems with a level of depth and breadth that few of their single-job peers can match.

This pursuit of mastery also brings a surprising byproduct: increased self-confidence. As they navigate the complexities of dual roles, the overemployed begin to recognise their own capacity for growth, adaptability, and resilience. Each successful project, each resolved crisis, each day that goes off without a hitch reinforces their belief in their abilities. For Maya, this self-assurance manifests as a calm confidence when tackling complex codebases; for Lucas, it's an intuitive understanding of market fluctuations that guides his recommendations. This inner confidence becomes a quiet strength, a conviction that they can handle the demands of their roles with poise and skill, no matter how challenging the day might be.

However, the road to mastery is not without its challenges. The pace of overemployment can lead to moments of overwhelm, a sense that they're constantly pushing their limits. For every moment of triumph, there are moments of doubt, times when Maya and Lucas question whether they can keep up with the relentless pace. Maya recalls a week when her deadlines collided, forcing her to work late into the night on one project while simultaneously fielding last-minute requests from her other job. The strain was palpable, a visceral reminder that mastery demands sacrifices. But for those who persevere, these difficult moments serve as rites of passage, experiences that test their resolve and ultimately make them stronger.

Moreover, this pursuit of mastery often leads the overemployed to view their roles through a lens of continual improvement, constantly seeking ways to optimise, streamline, and innovate. They become experimenters, constantly refining their processes to achieve better results with less effort. For Lucas, this means building automated models that save hours of repetitive analysis, while Maya has developed custom scripts that accelerate her coding workflow. These small efficiencies add up, allowing them to stay ahead of the demands of both jobs while freeing up mental space for strategic thinking. Over time, this habit of optimisation becomes a mindset, a way of approaching work that values efficacy over mere completion, insight over routine, and precision over volume.

Yet, for all the skill gains, the overemployed know that mastery requires a delicate balance. The challenge isn't just about acquiring new knowledge but knowing when to rest, when to step back, and when to push forward. This balance is essential for maintaining a sustainable path to mastery, ensuring that they don't sacrifice long-term growth for short-term gains. Maya has learned to build rest into her routine, dedicating weekends to personal projects and hobbies that reignite her creativity, reminding her that life is more than the sum of her professional achievements. Lucas has adopted a similar approach, setting aside time for hobbies that keep his mind sharp without the weight of work-related expectations. For both, this balance is a form of self-care, a way to ensure that their pursuit of mastery enhances rather than depletes their sense of self.

In the end, the pursuit of mastery within the context of overemployment becomes a journey not just of skill acquisition but of self-discovery. The overemployed learn not only what they are capable of professionally but who they are as individuals—their resilience, their adaptability, and their unique perspectives. They emerge from this journey not just as experts in their fields but as individuals who have tested, proven, and redefined their own potential. The mastery they attain is more than technical; it's personal, a testament to their willingness to push beyond limits, to embrace complexity, and to pursue growth in a way that transcends traditional career paths.

This is the essence of overemployment as a path to mastery: it's a crucible that forges not just skills but a new way of seeing the world, one that values depth, resilience, and the pursuit of excellence above all else. For those who choose this path, the reward is not just professional success but a profound, unshakeable confidence in their own capacity to learn, adapt, and thrive, no matter what challenges may come their way.

CHAPTER 21

ONE LAST SCORE

For many overemployed professionals, the dual-job lifestyle has an expiration date. While some embrace the unique challenge and rewards of a double life, others see it as a strategic phase, a chapter that will eventually close once they achieve financial freedom or hit their savings goals. In overemployment circles, this vision is known as "the endgame," the plan for an eventual exit that grants them the autonomy and financial security they've been working towards. Unlike conventional career paths, where freedom is often tied to retirement decades down the line, the overemployed aim to exit much sooner, seeking a path that aligns with their goals and aspirations.

The endgame isn't simply about amassing wealth; it's about creating a lifestyle where time, choice, and personal values are no longer dictated by employers but by the overemployed themselves. It's a long game of planning, discipline, and sacrifice, one that requires focus on both the present demands of dual employment and the future vision of a life beyond it. For those with a clear plan, overemployment becomes a bridge—a phase they endure not just for the paycheck but for the promise of a life lived on their terms.

Naomi, a senior software developer, balances roles at a fast-paced tech company and a remote consulting firm. To Naomi, overemployment is a temporary strategy to fund a very specific dream: buying a homestead in rural Oregon, where she plans to build a small farm, run freelance projects, and live off the land. Every late night, every back-to-back meeting, and every project she completes brings her a step closer to this vision of freedom. She has an endgame fund, a carefully structured savings account where she deposits a fixed percentage of her income from both jobs, tracking her progress toward the day she'll say goodbye to her dual roles. For Naomi, this endgame isn't just a plan—it's her motivation, a reason to push through the exhaustion and stay focused amidst the demands of both jobs.

For others, the endgame is less about physical freedom and more about financial security. Jordan, a financial analyst, views overemployment as a way to fast-track his investment portfolio, aiming to reach financial independence by the age of forty. He's meticulous in his planning, investing carefully and strategically in diversified assets, viewing his second income as fuel for early retirement. While his peers are content with traditional savings accounts and slow-growing portfolios, Jordan's dual income allows him to take calculated risks, building a safety net that will eventually allow him to step away from both jobs and live off his investments. For Jordan, each paycheck is a ticket to freedom, a reminder that he's building a life where he won't be tethered to any employer.

This pursuit of an endgame adds a layer of intentionality to every decision the overemployed make. It shapes how they spend, how they save, and even how they work. Each project completed, each deadline met, isn't just another item crossed off the list—it's a milestone, a building block in a larger vision. Overemployed professionals like Naomi and Jordan have a different relationship with their income; it's not simply money earned but a resource strategically allocated to fuel their futures. This financial discipline is key, and for many, it's what keeps them grounded, a reminder that they're working for a purpose far greater than a paycheck.

Yet, planning for the endgame isn't simply a matter of saving and investing; it's also about knowing when to step back, when to let go, and when to trust that they've achieved enough. Many overemployed individuals struggle with the concept of "enough," the elusive point where financial security meets personal satisfaction. For some, the allure of dual incomes creates a cycle of dependency, a fear that stepping away from one job will disrupt the security they've built. They worry that without the buffer of a second income, they'll lose the momentum they've worked so hard to maintain.

This sense of attachment can make the final exit feel daunting. For individuals like Naomi, there's an emotional weight to leaving one of her jobs, a sense that she's giving up a hard-won advantage. She describes it as a "phantom dependency," a belief that her dual roles are the foundation of her security, even though her savings and investments are well within her goals. To ease this transition, she's created a "soft exit" plan—a gradual wind-down where she plans to take freelance projects to replace her second income, allowing her to maintain a sense of productivity while slowly stepping away from her current roles. This phased approach provides a psychological buffer, a way to let go without feeling like she's abandoning her progress.

For others, like Jordan, the exit requires a more abrupt shift. He's scheduled his final "walk-away" date for his fortieth birthday, a clear milestone that serves as both a goal and a line in the sand. He's prepared for this transition meticulously, with a detailed financial blueprint, an exit fund, and a plan for the years to come. The clarity of this end date brings him a sense of relief, a countdown that reminds him each day that he's moving toward his freedom.

While each individual's endgame differs, the underlying philosophy is the same: the overemployed see their dual roles as tools, not destinations. They've reframed work as a vehicle for autonomy, a method to achieve a life that's defined by choice rather than obligation. Their relationship with work is fundamentally different from that of traditional employees; it's transactional, intentional, and purpose-driven. For them, the endgame isn't about climbing a career ladder or accumulating job titles—it's about building a foundation that supports their dreams, their values, and their ultimate vision of freedom.

In the end, the pursuit of an endgame requires more than just financial planning—it demands a mindset of resilience, patience, and self-discipline. It's a journey of endurance, a quiet but unyielding commitment to a future they can truly call their own. And when the day finally comes to step away, to close the chapter on overemployment, the rewards extend far beyond money. For Naomi, it will be the satisfaction of walking across her own land, of watching her dreams take root in the soil. For Jordan, it will be the thrill of realising he's no longer bound by financial constraints, that he has earned the right to choose his own path.

The endgame, for the overemployed, is a testament to the power of intention, a reminder that work can be a stepping stone rather than a destination. It's a vision of life as a canvas, where every project, every paycheck, and every sacrifice contributes to a masterpiece of autonomy and purpose. And for those who reach it, the endgame represents not just the end of overemployment, but the beginning of a life lived fully, freely, and entirely on their terms.

CHAPTER 22

REDEFINING OUR RELATIONSHIP WITH WORK

Overemployment, for many, is not just a financial strategy or a temporary lifestyle—it's a form of quiet rebellion. By rejecting the conventions of a single, all-consuming job, the overemployed challenge the very structures that define work, questioning the societal norms that bind identity, self-worth, and success to a solitary professional role. For them, work isn't a monolithic identity but a toolkit, a series of interchangeable functions they can reshape, repurpose, and, ultimately, control. In this chapter, we explore how overemployment becomes a deeply personal, almost philosophical act of resistance—a redefinition of work that frees the individual from the constraints of traditional employment.

In many ways, overemployment is a direct response to the "work as identity" culture that has become the norm in modern society. For decades, the idea that one's career is the central axis of life has been so pervasive that it's gone largely unchallenged. Job titles, promotions, and office dynamics often consume conversations, and success is measured by metrics tied closely to one's professional output. The overemployed, however, have chosen a different path, one that prioritises autonomy over title, income over status, and personal freedom over workplace loyalty. For them, the job is a means to an end, a way to finance a life that exists outside the confines of any single role.

Bailey, a marketing strategist, has embraced overemployment not out of financial need but out of a desire to regain control over her life. In her previous job, Bailey often found herself frustrated with the limited scope of her role, the rigid expectations, and the unspoken rules that stifled her creativity. Overemployment, with its blend of diverse responsibilities and flexible structure, gave her the autonomy she craved. By balancing two roles, she's been able to cultivate a unique perspective on her industry, viewing each job as an opportunity to explore, experiment, and grow. For Bailey, overemployment is more than a work strategy—it's a reclamation of her professional agency, a choice that allows her to define her career on her own terms.

But this quiet rebellion goes beyond personal autonomy; it challenges the very notion of "job loyalty" that has underpinned the traditional employer-employee relationship for generations. Overemployed individuals are often seen as mercenaries, professionals who are unwilling to give their undivided loyalty to a single employer. And in some ways, this is true. The overemployed don't see themselves as loyal to a company; they see themselves as loyal to their own values, their own vision of a fulfilling life. This shift from company loyalty to self-loyalty is a radical reorientation, a statement that they value their independence and personal goals above the company's bottom line.

For Ethan, a software engineer juggling two development gigs, this detachment from traditional job loyalty has been transformative. In his first few months of overemployment, Ethan struggled with the guilt of not being fully "committed" to either employer. But as he continued to navigate his dual roles, he says, "I realised that my sense of guilt was rooted in an outdated mindset." One that placed his employer's needs above his own. Over time, he came to see that his loyalty belonged not to a company but to himself, his goals, and his vision for a life where work served him, not the other way around. This detachment has given him a sense of freedom, an ability to navigate his jobs without the emotional weight that often comes with corporate loyalty. I come and go as I please now, and I do a better job because of it. I don't spend so much time worrying about how I'm perceived, or asking am I doing enough?"

For overemployed individuals, this redefinition of loyalty also leads to a redefinition of success. Where traditional career paths often equate success with title, position, and corporate approval, the overemployed measure success in terms of autonomy, financial stability, and personal satisfaction. Their goals are not tied to promotions or corporate milestones but to their own ambitions, dreams, and values. This shift allows them to find meaning in their work without being confined by the metrics of any one job.

For many, the true success lies in the ability to walk away from a role if it no longer serves them, to pivot when they choose, and to prioritise their own well-being over a company's agenda.

This quiet rebellion against the corporate structure also cultivates a mindset of self-reliance, a belief that they are responsible for their own growth, development, and security. Overemployed professionals like Bailey and Ethan take charge of their own professional trajectory, continuously learning, adapting, and pushing themselves in ways that a single role would never allow. They view work as a personal resource, a platform for skill-building and experimentation rather than a fixed career ladder. This mindset fosters a resilience, an inner fortitude that allows them to navigate the uncertainties of multiple roles with confidence and adaptability.

But redefining the relationship with work also brings its own challenges. For those who reject the traditional work paradigm, there's a sense of "otherness," a feeling of being on the fringes of society's norms. The overemployed often find themselves navigating a world where their choices are met with confusion or judgment, where colleagues, friends, and family members may question the ethics or sustainability of their lifestyle. This can create a sense of isolation, a feeling that they're pursuing a path few understand or appreciate. However, for those who embrace this lifestyle fully, this sense of otherness becomes a source of strength, a reminder that they are living by their own rules, charting a course that is as unique as it is self-determined.

Overemployment also changes how these individuals view risk and reward. They are no longer tied to a single paycheck or beholden to one company's fortunes, but instead have diversified their income and their professional security. This diversification creates a sense of financial resilience, a stability that allows them to take risks, explore new fields, and even pivot industries if they choose. For many, this is the ultimate reward—not just the financial gain, but the freedom to explore, experiment, and evolve without the fear of losing everything in one job's downturn. They've effectively become their own safety net, creating a stability that is self-sustained and self-defined.

In redefining their relationship with work, the overemployed have unlocked a way of life that feels radical, almost subversive. They've unbound themselves from the constraints of traditional employment, creating a model where work is flexible, responsive, and adaptable to their needs. For them, work is no longer a fixed identity or a lifelong commitment, but a fluid construct, a resource they control rather than one that controls them. This is the essence of their quiet rebellion—a refusal to let their lives be dictated by job titles or corporate structures, a rejection of the idea that success must come at the cost of personal freedom.

In the end, the overemployed are more than just workers with two jobs—they're pioneers, individuals who are reshaping the future of work itself. They've shown that employment can be plural, that loyalty can be self-directed, and that success can be defined not by society but by one's own terms. Their quiet rebellion is a testament to the human capacity for reinvention, a reminder that work, when viewed through the lens of autonomy and intention, can be a pathway to liberation, a tool for self-realisation, and ultimately, a choice rather than an obligation.

CHAPTER 23

NEW WAYS TO MEASURE SUCCESS

In this particular market, success is no longer defined by traditional metrics—promotions, corporate titles, and employer loyalty. Instead, success is measured by the personal milestones they achieve, the autonomy they cultivate, and the legacy they create outside of their roles. Overemployment is, at its core, a journey of self-empowerment, one where they set the rules, design the roadmap, and define the end goals. And as they near the endgame, the overemployed often find themselves reflecting on the unconventional life they've built, questioning what it means to truly succeed in a world where their careers no longer hold them captive.

For many, the legacy they're building isn't about the work itself—it's about what the work enables. The overemployed see their roles as fuel for the life they want to lead, not as the destination itself. They're working for something greater, something rooted in freedom, creativity, and purpose. Liam is a software architect who's been balancing dual roles for nearly five years. To Liam, overemployment has always been a path to financial freedom, a means to pursue his lifelong dream of opening a community art centre. Each project completed, each performance review aced, and each milestone hit brings him closer to a vision that has nothing to do with tech, coding, or software solutions. Liam's legacy, in his mind, isn't built within his jobs—it's built outside them, in a world where his time and resources can be directed toward creative, community-focused endeavours.

For individuals like Liam, the true success of overemployment is found in the ability to design a life that aligns with their values, dreams, and ambitions beyond the workplace. They are investing their time and energy in pursuits that aren't captured in job descriptions or CVs. Whether it's a dream of traveling the world, launching a passion project, or securing generational wealth for their families, the overemployed treat their dual roles as a foundation for something more meaningful, something deeply personal that doesn't rely on any company's validation or approval. This redefinition of success transforms overemployment from a survival tactic into a legacy-building tool, a way to fund lives that are rich not in job titles but in experiences, connections, and achievements that extend far beyond the workplace.

Yet, as they carve out this new definition of success, the overemployed are often confronted with a deeper question: What happens to their sense of identity when work is no longer central to who they are? For many, this is a profound shift, a realisation that by decoupling self-worth from work, they've unlocked a kind of freedom they hadn't known was possible. Dave, an operations manager with two jobs in logistics, describes this experience as "a release from obligation." By embracing overemployment, he's freed himself from the need to impress, outperform, or define himself through his career alone. He no longer feels pressure to climb a corporate ladder or seek validation through promotions. Instead, he finds value in what he creates, what he learns, and how he spends his time outside of work. For Dave, success isn't about recognition from employers; it's about building a life that feels authentic and self-directed, a life where work is a resource, not a ruling force.

This new definition of success also brings a distinct relationship with time, one where the overemployed become highly attuned to how they spend each hour, day, and year. With two jobs, every minute becomes an investment, a decision between earning, resting, or creating. And for those nearing the end of their overemployment journey, time itself becomes the ultimate currency, something they cherish and protect fiercely. Rather than spending decades tied to a single role or employer, the overemployed have compressed their career into a span of intense, focused years, knowing that each hour of dual work is a step toward a life where time belongs solely to them. This perspective transforms their understanding of time from something to be spent into something to be valued and, eventually, reclaimed.

Maya, a data scientist who balances dual roles, took on the extra stress and gave up free time to fund her dream of retiring before the age of forty. For Maya, success means having the freedom to decide how to spend her time without financial dependency on anyone else. Every time she's skipped a weekend outing or worked late into the night, she's reminded herself that this sacrifice isn't about pleasing a manager or proving her dedication. It's about building a life where her time, her most precious asset, is fully her own. This mindset shift, from working to earn time to working to own time, is a radical transformation that challenges conventional career goals. In many ways, Maya's version of success is a direct challenge to the norm—it's a legacy of autonomy, a statement that life is measured not by output but by the freedom to live as one chooses.

This philosophy, this redefined vision of success, sets the overemployed apart from traditional career paths. They aren't looking for accolades or titles; they're looking for something intangible yet profoundly rewarding—a life rich in experiences, self-mastery, and the knowledge that they've built something of their own. For many, this means redefining even their daily routines, investing time in skills or hobbies that have nothing to do with work. They might pursue creative interests, develop personal talents, or build relationships that transcend professional networks. Liam, for example, spends hours each week practicing photography, honing a skill that brings him joy and fulfilment outside the screen-bound world of software. This pursuit isn't tied to his career or financial goals; it's a part of his legacy, a reminder that success includes nurturing all parts of oneself, not just the productive or profitable parts.

This redefinition of success also creates a ripple effect, inspiring those around them to consider new perspectives on work and life. Friends, family, and even colleagues begin to see that overemployment is more than just a hustle; it's a reimagining of what life can be when work is repurposed as a stepping stone to autonomy. Overemployed individuals often become examples within their circles, showing that it's possible to break free from the constraints of a single career path and build a multi-faceted life that's as fulfilling as it is unconventional. They become reminders that success doesn't have to mean sacrifice, that ambition doesn't have to equate to burnout, and that true achievement can be found in the spaces between work— spaces filled with creativity, connection, and choice.

In the end, the overemployed leave behind more than financial security; they leave a legacy of resilience, creativity, and self-determination. They've shown that success can be a personal narrative, a story written in their own words, one that doesn't conform to the metrics of any job description. For them, overemployment isn't just about doubling their income—it's about doubling their lives, creating a legacy of freedom, choice, and self-expression. And for those who follow in their footsteps, the path they've paved is more than an alternative career model; it's an invitation to reimagine success, to build a life where work is just one part of a much richer, more meaningful story.

This legacy of the overemployed isn't captured in titles or job descriptions but in the lives they live on their own terms, in the memories they make, and in the freedom they've claimed. Their success is a silent yet powerful rebellion, a refusal to let work define them, and a testament to the extraordinary lives that can be built when one chooses to step off the beaten path.

CHAPTER 24

KEY TAKEAWAYS FOR AFICIONADOS

The ease with which traditional white collar workers have taken to overemployment, with its unique challenges and rewards, has illuminated a powerful truth about modern work: success is not a one-size-fits-all concept. The overemployed are rewriting the rules, crafting a future where work is reimagined as a flexible, personal resource rather than a defining element of identity. Their experiences serve as a roadmap for redefining success, autonomy, and the role of work in our lives. In this final chapter, we crystallise the core insights of the overemployed journey—a manifesto for those seeking freedom, purpose, and self-determination within and beyond their careers.

1. Work as a Means, Not an End

Overemployment is founded on the idea that work is a tool, not a destination. The overemployed use their roles strategically, not to climb traditional career ladders but to fuel their own personal and financial goals. This shift reframes work from an obligation into a resource—a transactional means to gain the autonomy, stability, and freedom they seek. For those who embrace this mindset, success becomes decoupled from titles, promotions, and external validation, allowing for a more fulfilling, self-directed life.

2. Mastery Through Multidimensional Learning

The overemployed have transformed the dual-job experience into an accelerated pathway for skill-building and self-mastery. By managing multiple roles, they develop not only job-specific skills but also meta-skills—time management, adaptability, strategic thinking—that enrich their professional and personal lives alike. This multi-layered learning amplifies their versatility, making them agile, capable, and ready to tackle challenges from multiple perspectives. In a world that increasingly values adaptability, the overemployed demonstrate that diverse experience is as valuable, if not more so, than traditional expertise.

3. Redefining Loyalty – Self-Commitment Over Company Commitment

In redefining loyalty, the overemployed shift their allegiance from a single employer to their own goals and values. By prioritising self-loyalty, they liberate themselves from the constraints of corporate loyalty, choosing instead to dedicate their time and energy to pursuits that genuinely serve their interests. This mindset fosters a healthy detachment, allowing them to navigate multiple roles without the emotional weight of corporate expectations. The overemployed remind us that loyalty to oneself is the highest form of commitment, creating a career path that reflects true personal agency.

4. Resilience and Boundaries as Essential Skills

Overemployment teaches a new kind of resilience, one built on boundaries and self-preservation. By balancing two roles, the overemployed learn to protect their time, their energy, and their mental well-being, setting clear boundaries that ensure sustainability. This resilience is not about enduring burnout but about managing resources wisely, knowing when to push forward and when to step back. Boundaries become the cornerstone of their success, empowering them to maintain long-term growth and avoid the pitfalls of overextension.

5. A New Financial Model – Wealth as Freedom, Not Security

For the overemployed, financial success isn't about accumulating wealth for security alone—it's about buying freedom. Every paycheck, every project completed, is a step toward a life where financial dependence on employers is reduced, and personal autonomy is enhanced. This new financial model focuses on building assets, reducing reliance on any one job, and creating an exit plan that leads to financial independence. In shifting their focus from income alone to wealth as a foundation for choice, the overemployed redefine financial success as the ability to walk away from work on their own terms.

6. The Power of Selective Identity

Overemployment offers a lesson in identity flexibility—the ability to shift between roles, functions, and personas without being tethered to any one. By avoiding a singular, work-based identity, the overemployed protect themselves from burnout, job dependency, and the hollowing effect of corporate roles that demand too much without giving enough back. This selective identity allows them to thrive across multiple domains, creating a layered, robust sense of self that extends beyond any single job or career. In doing so, they remind us that work should serve identity, not consume it.

7. A Legacy of Autonomy and Choice

Ultimately, overemployment is a pathway to autonomy, a means of reclaiming control over time, decisions, and life itself. The overemployed don't measure success by job titles or corporate accolades but by the freedom they've carved out to make choices on their own terms. This legacy of autonomy is the true endgame: a life where time belongs to them, where each decision is a personal choice rather than a corporate expectation, and where work is flexible, empowering, and deeply fulfilling. The overemployed have shown that true success is about more than income; it's about crafting a life rich in freedom, self-ownership, and personal meaning.

The Manifesto – Redefining Success and Work

The experiences of the overemployed highlight a new paradigm, one where work serves the individual, not the other way around. Their journey offers a manifesto for those seeking to reimagine their relationship with work:

1. **Let work serve your life, not define it.**
2. **Embrace flexibility and adaptability as sources of strength.**
3. **Build loyalty to your own values, ambitions, and dreams.**
4. **Value resilience and boundaries as essential tools for sustainable success.**
5. **Pursue financial freedom as a path to autonomy, not just security.**
6. **Reject identity solely tied to job titles; let identity be multidimensional.**
7. **Measure success in terms of freedom, purpose, and choice.**

The overemployed are showing us a radical new direction, one where success isn't measured by promotions or corporate loyalty but by the freedom to define one's own priorities and path. Their quiet revolution reveals that work can be more than a single, lifelong lane. It can be an adaptable tool—a resource for reaching financial independence, exploring new skills, and crafting a multifaceted life that reflects the complexity of personal ambition.

This movement asks us to rethink our assumptions about the purpose of work. Rather than a singular, all-consuming pursuit, employment becomes a flexible structure that can be shaped to support multiple goals. The overemployed reject the notion that work must be an identity; instead, they view it as a means to build something personal and enduring, a legacy that speaks to their individual values rather than corporate KPIs. They demonstrate that our relationship with work can be dynamic, allowing us to shift between roles, industries, or entirely new career arcs—all without sacrificing the larger vision of financial stability and personal growth.

Overemployment is an ongoing live exercise that is reshaping our relationship with productivity. It's also a refusal to let traditional metrics define worth. It offers a future where ambition is no longer confined to a single role or title, but becomes a more nuanced and multidimensional pursuit. For those who dare to deviate from the standard path, the rewards aren't just financial; they extend to a deeper kind of satisfaction—the pride of navigating multiple worlds, honing a variety of skills, and discovering a strength that thrives on adaptability.

Ultimately, the overemployment movement presents us with an alternative to the standard, linear work-life balance. It invites us to reconsider work itself as a vehicle not only for income but for freedom, exploration, and autonomy.

This model transcends the nine-to-five, turns the gig economy on its head, while empowering those who adopt it to take control of their time and, by extension, their lives.

In doing this, the overemployed have gifted us a blueprint for a more resilient, self-directed existence—one where success is self-defined and a rich, diverse life is the ultimate reward.

This page left intentionally blank to subvert audience expectations.

OVEREMPLOYED

OVEREMPLOYED: The Digital Workers' Movement Redefining *Business as Usual* in the Remote Work Age

Solar Storm Press
https://solarstorm.net.au/
reachout@solarstorm.net.au

ABOUT THE AUTHOR

Rob Hackney is a Melbourne author, comedian, and filmmaker. He is, in contrast to those depicted in this book, a little bit *under*employed, if anything.

@RobHackneyEsq

rob@robhackney.com / **robhackney.com**

www.ingramcontent.com/pod-product-compliance
Lightning Source LLC
Chambersburg PA
CBHW032003190326
41520CB00007B/337